SPIRITUAL REALITIES
AND THE
TRIBAL HEART

How to cleanse and restore your generational line

SUSAN BOWMAN

Spiritual Realities and the Tribal Heart
© Susan Bowman 2026

Published by Armour Books
P. O. Box 492, Corinda QLD 4075 Australia

Cover & interior design and typeset by Beckon Creative
Cover image: Giovanni_Cancemi | Depositphotos
Interior decals: Beckon Creative

ISBN: 978-1-923533-06-6

 A catalogue record for this book is available from the National Library of Australia

All rights reserved. No part of this publication may be reproduced, stored in, or introduced into a retrieval system, or transmitted, in any form, or by any means (electronic, mechanical, photocopying, recording or otherwise) without the prior written permission of the publisher.

Unless otherwise indicated all Scripture is from the New American Standard Bible. New American Standard Bible®, Copyright © 1960, 1962, 1963, 1968, 1971, 1972, 1973, 1975, 1977, 1995 by The Lockman Foundation. Used by permission. (www.Lockman.org)

Scripture quotations marked AMP are taken from the Amplified Version of the Bible Copyright © 2015 by The Lockman Foundation, La Habra, CA 90631. All rights reserved. www.lockman.org

Scripture quotations marked ESV are taken from the ESV® Bible (The Holy Bible, English Standard Version®), copyright © 2001 by Crossway, a publishing ministry of Good News Publishers. Used by permission. All rights reserved.

Scripture quotations marked GNT are from the Good News Translation in Today's English Version—Second Edition Copyright © 1992 by American Bible Society. Used by Permission.

Scripture quotations marked NIV are taken from the Holy Bible, New International Version®, NIV®. Copyright © 1973, 1978, 1984, 2011 by Biblica, Inc.™ Used by permission of Zondervan. All rights reserved worldwide. www.zondervan.com The "NIV" and "New International Version" are trademarks registered in the United States Patent and Trademark Office by Biblica, Inc.™.

Scripture quotations marked NLT are taken from the Holy Bible, New Living Translation, copyright 1996, 2004. Used by permission of Tyndale House Publishers, Inc., Wheaton, Illinois 60189. All rights reserved.

Also by Susan Bowman

In this series

The Quiet Heart:
A Foundational Guide to Inner Healing and Deliverance

The Performing Heart:
How to Escape the Trap of Relentless Performing and Enter the Security of God's Rest

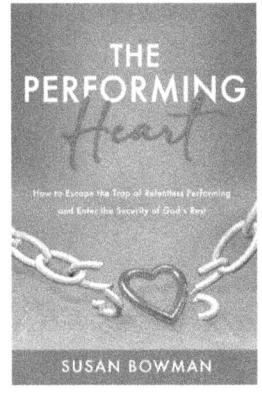

Dedicated to Sam Bowman, the best husband in the world.

CONTENTS

Acknowledgements   9

1. We All Begin Somewhere   11
   Study Guide 209

2. Is That You, God, or Just My Imagination?   21
   Study Guide 211

3. When an Elephant is Not an Elephant   37
   Study Guide 212

4. The Heart is a Boss   47
   Study Guide 213

5. You Are What Your Heart Believes   55
   Study Guide 214

6. Starting Point   67
   Study Guide 215

7. Mercy, Grace, and Weirdness Abound   75
   Study Guide 216

8. All Rise; Court is in Session   87
   Study Guide 217

9. The Framework   97
   Study Guide 218

10.	The Timeline	107
	Study Guide 219	
11.	Alligators and Carousels: Dismantling Tribal Heart Beliefs	119
	Study Guide 221	
12.	Reconciliation	129
	Study Guide 222	
13.	Wonders, Terrors, and Treasures	139
	Study Guide 224	
14.	The Blame Game	159
	Study Guide 225	
15.	Trades and Accusations	171
	Study Guide 227	
16.	Strategic Prayers and Protocols	183
	Study Guide 228	
17.	Justice is Served	193
	Study Guide 230	

Appendix	199
Works Cited	207
Study Guide and Small Group Discussion Questions	209
About the Author	231

ACKNOWLEDGEMENTS

Thank you for all you do.

Jim, Linda, Janie, Mary, Heather, and David

CHAPTER 1

WE ALL BEGIN SOMEWHERE

My intent with this book, the third in *The Heart* series, is to focus on your inheritance from your natural family. That inheritance includes much more than the stuff bequeathed to you. It includes your family's circumstances and environment at the time of your conception, birth, and childhood. It includes your family history.

For example, my mother was the first child of her immigrant parents. As a result, she inherited a very Italian way of life along with the American way of life. Her parents wanted her to be American, but she was living with completely Italian parents, extended family, and family friends. This environment and these circumstances strongly flavored how she viewed herself and life overall.

Such natural circumstances are easily observed. But, did you know that what your family believes about itself also has a profound effect on you?

You also are born into a family belief system. This family belief system is generations old and has a profound effect on how you understand yourself and life.

I had planned to straightforwardly teach you what I have learned about the family belief system. Then I was going to explain the different methods I use to bring awareness to this often-hidden set of beliefs and how these family-held beliefs affect you. Finally, I was going to offer a step-by-step approach to cleaning up any toxicity, so that the unique expression of God's goodness and greatness that is woven into the design of your people is restored and released. But as the poet Robert Burns said, "The best laid plans of mice and men often go astray."

When it dawned on me that some of my readers may be new to the idea of generational restoration, I decided to spend some time doing my best to explain a few things, while remaining true to writing a *how-to-restore-your-generational-line* book. For those of you who are well-versed in spiritual realities and have been exposed to the concept of generational restoration, feel free to visit any chapter you think may be relevant to your continuing education. I do recommend that you spend some time in the chapters concerning spiritual realities simply because many believers — even mature believers — tend to view these realities as literal when in most cases what we experience in the spiritual realm is supposed to be understood as symbolic. So, this chapter will be a brief overview of the generationally based, family belief system. Then the next few chapters will explain how spiritual realities are experienced and what to do with those realities. Please spend time practicing what you learn. You will be much better equipped to effectively apply the how-to guide that follows. I have included some suggested practices at the end of each chapter.

The Brief Overview

We Inherit Natural Circumstances

We are comfortable with the notion that being born into a wealthy family is an advantage that opens up opportunities. These opportunities are less available to those born into a family with fewer financial resources. For example, college students whose parents completed college are much more likely to graduate than students whose parents did not finish college. Consider these statistics from bestcolleges.com[1]:

Only 26% of first-generation college students finish their degree. Eighty-two percent of students with two parents who had earned bachelor's degrees or higher graduated with their bachelor's. First-generation college graduates made roughly $36,000 less than their non-first-generation counterparts.

Notice that not only is it much less likely that first-generation college students will graduate, they earn substantially less money when they do graduate. Why is that? One purely natural reason is because they are less likely to be connected to a network of successful people. It really *is* who you know. But there is another reason why success breeds success. A child born into a family that has for generations experienced success in the natural world will inherit the expectation of success. That expectation is woven into the family's belief system. The child not only inherits the advantages of his family's natural assets; he inherits the advantages of his family's belief system. The family shares the belief that *we are people who succeed.*

---

1 Jane Nam, "First-Generation College Student Facts," BestColleges, https://www.bestcolleges.com/research/first-generation-students-facts-statistics/ (accessed April 12, 2023)

We Inherit a Way of Believing

This shared way of believing is usually accepted and never spoken about, but it is a component deeply embedded into what I call the *tribal heart belief system*. The tribe I am referring to is your family extending back into time. Sometimes this tribe is called your *bloodline* or your *ancestors* or your *people*. The beliefs held within the heart of your tribe are handed down to each generation. Some ministers, myself included, believe that this tribal belief system is downloaded into the baby while in the womb. It certainly is transmitted via DNA[2], through eye-to-eye contact, by observing behaviors, by what is spoken within the family, and so on. Both the advantages of the tribal belief system and the disadvantages of the system are passed down.

> *You purchased people for God with Your blood from every tribe, language, people, and nation.*
>
> Revelation 5:9

The Tribal Heart Stores the Family Belief System

In order to change the beliefs stored within the tribal heart — so that the blessings and gifts placed within are released — you need to be able to locate and open that tribal heart belief system. Simply asking God to switch out fallen heart beliefs for godly heart beliefs, although not a bad idea, does not get the job done. This is because your heart stores your tribal belief system. And the heart is a storehouse that is not easily broken into.

> *Guard your heart above all else, for it determines the course of your life.*
>
> Proverbs 4:23 NLT

---

[2] Epigenetics is the study of how gene expression is altered by natural occurrences and environmental factors. These changes can be passed down the generational line.

The word translated *heart* is 'lēḇ' in Hebrew. 'Lēḇ' means the *physical heart*. The physical heart stores your personal belief system which is composed of the conclusions you have arrived at about yourself, others, and life. Your personal belief system is strongly influenced by your tribal belief system. What we believe at the heart level determines how we will interpret life. See *The Quiet Heart* and *The Performing Heart* for a detailed explanation and guides on managing your heart.

Once you do manage to unlock the storehouse of your heart, the ungodly beliefs hidden inside need to be identified and removed so that the godly treasure within may be accessed. This is not an impossible or even difficult process. But it is a process that needs to be learned, practiced, and applied.

The Blessings Within the Storehouse

Every generational line carries two types of blessings: the blessing of righteousness and the blessing of design.

The Blessing of Righteousness

Arthur Burk in *Relentless Generational Blessings* describes the blessing of righteousness as "God bestowing tangible benefits on a person or group of people as a result of a righteous act done by someone in a prior generation."[3] These blessings are deposited upon the generational line. You may come upon such blessings as you are restoring your bloodline. When you do, simply ask the Lord to release the blessing to you and your descendants as is appropriate. These are wonderful blessings and help us appreciate our bloodline.

---

3   Arthur Burk, *Relentless Generational Blessings*, (Whittier, California, Plumbline Ministries, 2003), 17.

The Blessing of Design

> *Adah gave birth to Jabal; he was the father of those who live in tents and have livestock. His brother's name was Jubal; he was the father of all those who play the lyre and flute. As for Zillah, she also gave birth to Tubal-cain, the forger of all implements of bronze and iron…*
>
> Genesis 4:20–22

The blessing of design is the more important blessing because God has woven into each and every tribe some expression of Himself and of heaven. This blessing is embedded into your natural and spiritual DNA. God has given it without revocation, so no matter how far off the rails your tribe may have gone, the blessing of design remains.

> *… for the gifts and the calling of God are irrevocable.*
>
> Romans 11:29

Now accessing and releasing that blessing of design can be a challenge. Helping you learn how that is done is why I am writing this book.

Generational restoration is a slow walk with God as He makes us aware of why and what our people believe. But we can speed up the restoration process by intentionally seeking to uncover the tribal heart belief system, and then investing the time to engage with, dismantle, and rebuild that belief system.

I believe that learning the skills within this book and applying them is well worth the effort because any generational restoration you do will profoundly affect your life and the lives of the generations following you, your children, and your children's children.

Back To the Importance of Spiritual Realities

As I mentioned before, when I began writing this book my plan was to simply teach you how to conduct a generational cleanse and restoration. Then I realized that some readers may not be acquainted with spiritual realities. I recall a former pastor asking the congregation if any had ever cast out a demon. Sam was traveling, so I was the only person who raised a hand. Good thing I sat in the back! (I was a misfit in that very traditional church).

A practical understanding of how spiritual realities are discerned is necessary if you are going to successfully restore your generational line. The beliefs held within a tribal heart got their start so many generations ago — usually because of some traumatic experience — that the real reason behind what and why your family believes the things it does has been lost. As your tribe responded to some ancient traumatic event, a perception of who they were as a people emerged. The tribe began to see others and even life itself through the lens of this traumatic event.

So, the reason why your tribe believes what it believes is lost to time. But there is another layer that makes cracking the storehouse of tribal heart beliefs challenging. Because the original event was traumatic and the decisions resulting from it painful, the tribe buried what really happened under a dreadful fear, vowing to never connect with the beliefs emerging from the trauma. Only the Holy Spirit, who knows all things, is able to reveal to you the entirety of your tribe's heart beliefs. Do not worry. Jesus promises us that:

> *"the Spirit of truth ... will guide you into all the truth."*
>
> John 16:13

Godly Spiritual Discernment

It is good to know that the Spirit of truth will guide us, but *how* does He guide us into all truth? What does the truth about the forgotten, and usually hidden, past look like when we seek that truth? How do we recognize the difference between the Lord showing us something and our own imaginations? Those are very good questions that I will attempt to answer in the following chapters.

I do not want you to undertake generational restorations spiritually blind. So, let's begin by exploring some of the spiritual realities that you will encounter, as well as how you will experience those realities, as you work alongside the Holy Spirit to restore your bloodline.

> *But if any of you lacks wisdom, let him ask of God, who gives to all generously and without reproach, and it will be given to him.*
>
> James 1:5

Practice

1. Reflect on your family's history (e.g., cultural background, economic status). Journal any recurring patterns and ask the Holy Spirit if they reflect tribal beliefs about identity, relationships, or life.

2. Set aside 10 minutes in a quiet space. Read Proverbs 4:23 aloud, then pray: "Lord, my heart is a storehouse of personal and tribal beliefs. I invite Your Spirit of truth to gently reveal one belief hidden in my tribal heart. Show me how it shapes my life and how to align it with Your truth." Journal any impressions, emotions, or memories that arise. Repeat this prayer daily for a week, noting patterns or insights.

3. Imagine your tribal heart as a literal storehouse. Sketch or describe this storehouse, asking yourself if it is locked or asking what is inside. Reflect on what might be stored there — both godly treasures (blessings) and ungodly beliefs. Pray, asking the Holy Spirit to guide you in opening this storehouse. Journal one step you feel led to take to begin accessing its contents.

CHAPTER 2

IS THAT YOU, GOD, OR JUST MY IMAGINATION?

But a natural person does not accept the things of the Spirit of God, for they are foolishness to him; and he cannot understand them, because they are spiritually discerned.

1 Corinthians 2:14–16

THERE ARE THREE SIGNIFICANT BELIEFS that are hidden within a tribal heart.

1. Identity – who we are as a people.
2. Relationships – how others perceive us and will treat us.
3. Life – how life treats us as a people.

Uncovering these beliefs will take time and patience on your part. It can be a messy and often confusing journey during which you will encounter spiritual realities that may make you uncomfortable and, then again, may delight you. But discovering and releasing the beauty and glory that God has invested into your bloodline is well worth any effort. Every tribe carries within its spiritual DNA unique expressions of God's glory and goodness that are sorely needed in our world.

To uncover these most important beliefs so that the gifting on your tribe is restored and released requires that you work alongside the Holy Spirit. Keep in mind that the Holy Spirit reveals the truth in many ways. A common way that He speaks to us is through metaphor, simile, and symbolism. We will explore that a little later. In this chapter, I want to look at how we experience spiritual realities. Spiritual realities are experienced through our senses — hearing, seeing, feeling, smelling, and tasting. You will need to practice discerning spiritual realities and receiving information from God through your natural senses. We only learn by practicing.

As you learn your way around the spiritual realm, you will also be growing in your understanding of how God communicates.

God's Voice, the Spiritual Realm, and Seeing

I was praying with a man who came to me wanting to learn how to apply the healing techniques found in my previous *Heart* books to his counseling practice. In my opinion, the very best way to learn how the techniques work is to apply them to yourself. He was willing to learn by working on his own heart beliefs. One issue he brought up immediately was the nagging belief that he could not hear God's voice. I was taken by surprise because he had described in detail the godly visions he regularly saw. As we worked together, the Holy Spirit revealed that he had a heart belief which was blocking his ability to hear the voice of God. So, God was bypassing that belief by talking to him through visions. My friend could not hear God's voice, because of a blockage in his belief system, but he could very clearly see God's voice.

All the people saw the thunder...

Exodus 20:18 ESV

> *Then Elisha prayed and said, "Lord, please, open his eyes so that he may see." And the Lord opened the servant's eyes, and he saw; and behold, the mountain was full of horses and chariots of fire all around Elisha.*
>
> 2 Kings 6:17

I believe seeing into the spirit realm is something all of us can do if we will close our eyes and intentionally look, praying, "Lord, please open my eyes." Let's stop here and pray that now.

> *Lord God, before I ask You to open my eyes so that I may see into the spiritual realm, I submit my senses to the Holy Spirit. If my natural senses are defiled in any way, either by my actions or those of my ancestors, I repent and ask for forgiveness. I ask the Lord Jesus by the power of His blood to activate the repentance I have just spoken and release forgiveness to me. Please cleanse my senses and make it safe for me to experience spiritual realities. I ask Holy Spirit to guide me as I learn and grow in my ability to discern spiritual realities. Please teach me how to see into the realm of the spirit.*

Learning to see in the spirit realm is an important skill that will come in very handy as you are restoring your bloodline. As a rule, when you look with intention, you will see a picture or a short scene. Sometimes, the picture you see will be one object or a person. Sometimes, a scene will appear. Often, what you see will repeat until you accept that you really are seeing something. At that point, ask the Lord to explain. The reason you will often need an explanation is because much of what you see will be in the form of a metaphor, simile, or a symbol and all need interpretation, so it is wise to avoid jumping to conclusions. In Daniel 8:15, Daniel saw visions that made no sense to him, so he asked for an interpretation.

> *When I, Daniel, had seen the vision, I sought to understand it …*

Most of the time, you will see your visions within your mind. Opened-eye visions are less common. From time to time, visions may come to you unsolicited, but when you are engaged in a generational restoration you will be like Daniel who was seeking information by intentionally looking into the spirit.

> *Now these were the visions in my mind as I lay on my bed: I was looking, and behold…*
>
> Daniel 4:10

Some people have been taught to distrust their imagination. The imagination is the ability to image something within the mind and it is a gift from God. Like all things in this fallen world, this ability has been misused. Isn't it time to use it for good? God gave us our ability to see within our minds. One way He speaks to us is by using this ability to see images within our minds.

Impressions and Glimpses

Oftentimes, seeing in the spirit is not nearly as clear as seeing in the natural. Many of us see spiritual realities by catching glimpses of vague impressions. Seeing a fleeting impression is the most common way that I see in the spirit whenever I close my eyes and intentionally look. Impressions are easy to dismiss because they are vague and seemingly random. If you are working alone, I suggest writing down your impressions so that you may ask the Lord to help you understand what He is showing you. Do not fall into the fallacy of believing that one way of seeing is more important than another. Opened-eye visions, closed-eye visions, and impressions are equally valid ways of seeing in the spiritual realm.

God Uses What You Know

When God speaks to you through a vision, He will use what is familiar to you. He will use what you know as He communicates with you. For example, I live in a community that is crazy about college football. The mascot for our championship football team is an elephant. If I see an elephant in a vision, I will ask God why He is bringing up football, which for me is a very big subject encompassing my university, my community, and my culture. God knows that I will interpret a vision of an elephant through that lens. In all likelihood, elephants do not mean championship football to you. For those raised in India, elephants do not bring American football to mind. In that culture, elephants are symbols of good luck, power, strength, and royalty as well as being associated with both the Hindi and Buddhist religions. Or, just to mix things up a bit, perhaps this saying will come to mind if you see the image of an elephant: *No one wants to talk about the elephant in the room.*

My point is this: Whatever elephants mean to you is what is important. Just keep in mind that God will not speak to you in some unknowable way that is outside of your experience. He will use the objects, customs, and people familiar to you. He uses your everyday experiences and environment. That does not mean that you will not see weird things in the spirit realm. Once while working on a project in the courts of heaven, I saw a giant shaggy monster that meant nothing to me, but the person I was working with recognized as a spirit called Behemoth. It looked rather like an overgrown Wookie from Star Wars and had no bearing on the work we were doing. The courts of heaven are often busy. But that is a topic for another chapter.

When doing work within the spirit realm, keep in mind that the overall meaning of what you are seeing is what is most important. Try to avoid overthinking the visions. Much like dreams, the details are often there for context.

But What Does It Mean?

We better talk about interpreting before we go any further. At a recent meeting of my church, I was looking and listening in the spirit during worship, wondering if the Lord had anything to say to any of us. As worship ended, I saw in my mind a picture of a young turnip plant and heard the words, "I feel like a turnip." That probably sounds silly to you. It sounded silly to me, but rather than miss what God was saying, I risked telling the group what I had seen and heard. My immediate thought was that feeling like a turnip meant that someone was struggling with the belief that they were stupid. Have you heard the expression, 'I haven't just fallen off the turnip truck'? It means I am not naïve, so don't try to take advantage of me.

My husband thought of this saying, 'You can't squeeze blood out of a turnip,' which means that you cannot get something from a person, especially money, if they do not have it. We tossed around possible interpretations while the woman the message was for researched turnips on the internet. Finally, her face wreathed in smiles, she reported that turnips are very nutritious and healthy. Eating clean and healthy food is very important to her. I said that the plant I had seen was a young healthy plant. She understood the message to mean that she was being planted in a new place where she could be happy and healthy. Here is some backstory. She had been forced to move and members of our church had offered her a place on their farm. That morning was her first day in her new home. The young, very green turnip plant I saw was an encouraging message of hope to her.

Notice that Sam and I both interpreted the message through our particular filters. We were both wrong. Receiving information from God is not hard once you know how that works, but accurate interpretation is a whole other thing. I have lost count of the times I have misinterpreted a vision or other message during a prayer session. You are probably wondering if misinterpretation is so easy, how can you guard against it?

Please take note that neither Sam nor I insisted that our interpretations were right. We offered them as possibles to be examined in the light of the Lord. So first, I suggest that you get comfortable with being wrong.

How to Guard Against Misinterpretations

1. Accept that your interpretation might be wrong.

2. Accept that all interpretation belongs to God, according to Joseph in Genesis 40:8. So invite the Lord to advise you as you search for the meaning.

3. If the message is for you, listen to your inner man. That is, trust that feeling on the inside of you. That feeling is the Holy Spirit saying *yea* or *nay* to the interpretation. We describe this feeling to children as a cold yukky or a warm fuzzy. Go with the warm fuzzy.

4. Keep in mind that just because an interpretation makes sense, that does not mean that it is correct. Blood from a turnip and falling off a turnip truck made sense, but neither were right. So, trust your inward witness over your intellect.

5. Trust your inward witness over someone else's opinionated interpretation. If someone's interpretation makes sense, but does not feel right, then it is not right.

6. Do not be discouraged if you do not receive an interpretation immediately. A student of mine reported hearing 'nothing' whenever she asked her heart what she believed. This went on for several weeks and both of us were baffled. Eventually, in the middle of a prayer session with a completely different person, I realized that *nothing* was what my student believed. She believed within her heart she was a nothing and that was why she was not cherished as a child.

7. If you are helping someone interpret a dream, vision, or something they heard in the spirit, do not insist on being right. If your

interpretation does not feel right to the one you are helping, leave it alone.

Let's move on to another way that God communicates with us.

God's Voice, the Spiritual Realm, and Hearing

Oftentimes, when you are looking and listening intentionally in the spirit you will hear a single word, a phrase, a bible verse, or even a song. Occasionally, people report hearing odd sounds such as a bell ringing, the tramping of feet, or shouting. Remember what I said about how easy it is to dismiss those fleeting visions I call impressions? Much like impressions, what you hear in the spirit is easy to dismiss or ignore. Train yourself to lean into impressions *and* into the sounds you hear in the spirit. All of us tend to overlook the quieter ways that the Lord communicates. We really only pay attention if He hits us in the face with a pizza. And I think we all want Him to talk to us loudly since paying such close attention takes time and practice. Part of the problem is our habit (we do not even realize we have this habit) of ignoring what we do not understand. So keep in mind that, like impressions, words or sounds should be accepted and prayed over for interpretation.

> *My sheep hear My voice, I know them, and they follow Me.*
>
> John 10:27 NKJV

There are a couple of challenges to hearing in the spirit realm. These challenges apply to seeing as well, but let's look at them from the hearing angle, then you can apply the principles to the visions you see.

Evil spirits may attempt to give you deceptive visions, but they are much more likely to use language against you. If you do see unpleasant visions or hear confusing or unpleasant things, ask the Lord to explain. Sometimes an unpleasant vision is not from the enemy. Sometimes a vison reveals what we believe. (Recall my student who saw and heard *nothing* when she asked her heart what she believed). What we hear also may reveal a heart belief that is interfering with your ability to enjoy God. That same student, when we were practicing hearing God by asking Him a question and then writing what we heard in response, wrote 'pray harder and pray more.' This response made her feel very anxious and she exclaimed that she already talked to God all day! What more could He want? At the time, I thought maybe she had not heard God correctly, but later I realized that God was revealing to her what she believed. She had to work harder! Perform more and then maybe God would like her. He loves her and wants that heart belief corrected so that they can enjoy each other. But He cannot help her correct a painful heart belief if she is unaware of that painful heart belief.

God will reveal to you the damaging things that you believe. So, be sure to bring whatever you hear or see before the Lord and ask what and why questions. Asking God *what does it mean* and *why am I perceiving it* will become primary questions as you work with Him to restore your generational line.

Here is the second challenge. Evil spirits use language as a weapon. They lie, deceive, manipulate, and seduce with words. It is essential that you check everything you hear in the spirit. Ask the Lord to confirm what you hear in other ways. Make sure it aligns with God's revealed Word.

> *They aimed bitter speech as their arrows, to shoot from concealment at the innocent.*
>
> Psalm 64:3–4

Sometimes evil spirits will pretend to be God speaking to you. Just remember that God will never tell you to create a "new" gospel, to marry the pastor's spouse, or lash out at someone. The fruit of the Spirit is found in Galatians 5. Study that chapter so that you will not be deceived by what you hear in the spirit.

> *… we are not ignorant of his* [Satan's] *schemes.*
>
> 2 Corinthians 2:11

God's love is not weak or passive. Sometimes He will tell you to speak truth into hard situations. But He will not send you to others with a "word" for them that is manipulative, controlling, or motivated by fear. Ask the Lord to confirm what you hear for others (and yourself) in many different ways. This is to protect them from you (and you from you) in the event that you are deceived. Keep in mind the turnip vision. Sam and I both misunderstood the message. Only by talking it through were we able to arrive at the encouraging word God had for our friend.

God may speak a corrective word to you, but never to harm you. His motive is to rescue you and call you into maturity. He may tell you to separate from dangerous people. He may bring up challenging issues so that you will talk with Him about them. He will NOT send you into a foreign mission field without confirming such a call in a dozen different ways AND giving you a strong desire to go. Jesus warned us to:

> *"take care how you listen."*
>
> Luke 8:18

How you listen is important. Are you listening to hear what you want to hear? Are you listening without asking questions? Are you accepting what you hear without checking with the Lord?

Be very cautious when you hear something in the spirit. Ask the Lord to confirm what you hear in other ways to make sure the enemy is not involved. And if the enemy is involved, ask the Lord why.

Hearing may take place within a vision. But often, it stands alone. You may hear a single word or sound. You may hear a phrase. Remember that when you are cleansing your generational line, you are listening intentionally for God's guidance. You are asking Him to show you what you need to know and how to pray in order to release the goodness within your bloodline.

> *Now there was a disciple at Damascus named Ananias; and the Lord said to him in a vision, "Ananias."*
> *And he said, "Here I am, Lord."*
>
> Acts 9:10

God's Voice, Spiritual Realities, and Feeling

My friend called to report that her very sick brother was on his way to the hospital. She had just gotten off the phone with her distraught sister-in-law who had told her that the brother was so miserable that he wanted to die. Although my friend's voice was calm, I could feel how sad she was. When I assured her that I would pray for her brother and for her because I could feel her sadness, she broke down and cried. Please make a note. I felt her sadness by *feeling* her sadness. In other words, I felt sad too.

My son and I went to our covered mall to walk together. As we were leaving, a woman and her friend were wheeling a toddler into the mall. The toddler suddenly stiffened and began to cry. The women were baffled because the child had gone from happy to distressed — a distress that increased the closer they came the doors of the mall. I spoke silently into the spirit realm, informing any evil beings inside the mall that the child was off-limits. The child instantly stopped crying. My son asked me why we did not discern the presence of any evil spirits while walking in the mall and I reminded him that we are protected by a restraining order that I had asked God's courts to in put in place over the family.

I was given permission to use a quiet classroom in the back of the church since my office was too busy and noisy for thinking. As I settled in, I noticed that I felt jumpy and anxious. Since I had no reason to feel that way, I told the angels to remove any emotions leftover by anyone, to consecrate the room to the Lord's purposes, and fill it with heaven. My inexplicable nervousness disappeared. I was able to work peacefully.

My friend reported that she had begun dreading going to her church. She felt depressed and sad during the service. She started slipping out after worship. But even during worship, she felt dark and sad. She cried a lot. But as soon as she left the building, she felt fine. We prayed together and the Lord told us that the church was dying because the leadership had fallen to ambition. The humble acts of shepherding had been abandoned in order to seek promotion in the wider church world. My sensitive friend was discerning the state of her church by feeling it.

Feeling emotions is the number one way most people *unintentionally* discern the everyday spiritual realities surrounding them. Try to remember a time when you felt that something was off like I felt in that classroom. Perhaps when you entered a public place or when someone engaged with you, you felt like something was wrong. How did you feel that off-ness? Did you feel jumpy and nervous for no obvious reason?

The other day, I noticed that my heart rate was up. I felt tension in my chest. Since I had no reason to feel so jumpy, I asked Sam if he was anxious about anything. Sam denied feeling anxious, but sat next to me and poured out all the decisions that he was facing. Once he finished telling me all about it, we both felt better.

Have you ever felt anxious or rejected around someone before they have said or done anything? We often sense another person's emotional state by feeling what they are feeling. This can be confusing, because we automatically believe that anything we feel is ours.

Remember that one of the most important questions you can ask the Lord is why. Why do I feel this off-ness around so-and-so? Why do I feel anxious around her or him? Are You warning me about someone? Am I feeling what that person feels? Why am I uncomfortable in this place? What is really going on?

God may answer your questions by speaking to you or showing you a vision. If you still feel uncertain, ask Him to show you in other ways until you feel that certainty within you that is the witness of the Holy Spirit.

Not only do we discern information about other people by feeling it with our emotions, we may feel the presence of evil spirits. A primary way we discern the presence of a demon is by feeling a strong negative emotion such as fear or shame. Demons harvest the negative emotions of people. C. S. Lewis' *The Screwtape Letters* describes this demonic activity. Sometimes the demons gather up the negative emotions of people then off-load these random emotions onto someone else. This can create tremendous confusion, especially within a group, because what is being felt has no connection to reality. The good news is that we also are able to feel the presence of the Lord, His angels, and heaven.

Not only do we discern spiritual realities in our everyday life by feeling them, we also receive information about our generational line through our emotions. When intentionally seeking information about what the tribe believes within its heart, you may experience emotions. The most common emotions people feel during a generational restoration are shame, despair, hopelessness, grief, anger, hatred, and confusion. Sometimes people report feeling tightness in the chest, an upset stomach, headache, a choking sensation, or sudden exhaustion.

It is very easy for us to attribute any emotions we feel to ourselves. Do not forget that you are intentionally seeking information from the spirit realm. Anything you feel during a generational restoration session should be treated as a message that needs to be interpreted.

While you are seeking generational restoration, pay attention to your positive emotions also. When you have arrived at the truth, you may feel good or certain. You may feel like a burden has been lifted. You may feel what my ministry team likes to describe as a shift. These kinds of feelings help you know that you are on the right track.

God's Voice, Spiritual Realities, and Smelling and Tasting

One hot summer afternoon, a thin, dirty mother cat came begging at my door. Of course I fed her, but I wanted to locate her kittens. After eating, she wandered away and I followed at a distance. As we drew near to where she had hidden her litter, I began to smell baby powder. Wary of me, mother cat did not go directly to her kits, but set off in another direction. Instead of following her, I followed the smell which led me to a substantial junk pile inside a neighbor's carport. Crouching down, I peered into the dark. Three pairs of bright kitten eyes peered back. Mother cat joined me and we all went home together.

Discerning spiritual realities by smell and taste is rare for me personally. But it is a valid way that God speaks and one way that we may experience the spiritual realm. The presence of demons may be discerned by smelling a foul odor. The presence of unseen heavenly beings may be discerned by smelling a refreshing and lovely fragrance. Once, in a conference, my friend drew my attention to the fragrance of lilies coming from the spiritual realm. I had paid it no attention until she suggested that I breathe in the beautiful fragrance.

While participating in a generational restoration, smell and taste may be used to give you information. Remember to stop and ask God why you are tasting or smelling anything unusual.

I have covered quite a bit in this chapter. For some, the information is not new, but for others it is very new. Learning to be aware of spiritual realities takes two things. First, the willingness to learn. That may mean confronting any fear that you have about the spiritual realm. Second, it takes practice and practice and more practice. I believe we will be learning and honing these skills all of our lives. Let's ask God to help us.

> *Dear Lord, there is so much data coming into my senses just in the natural. I will need Your wisdom and help to sort out what is spiritual and what is not. I will need You to show me when the emotions I am feeling are my emotions, the emotions of another, or the emotions*

floating about in the environment. I am asking You to be my teacher. Please train me to be aware of spiritual realities and help me avoid being skeptical or afraid.

As I seek restoration for my bloodline, Lord, I ask that You provide me with the visions, sounds, feelings, smells, and tastes that are necessary to bring to light the heart beliefs of my people. Please be the interpreter of these spiritual realities. I submit my senses to You. I submit my understanding to You.

In Jesus' name, I pray. Amen

Practice

1. Close your eyes and imagine seeing the Cross. Do not worry if the image you see is vague. Now imagine the Lord Jesus joining you there. Engage your senses. Stay in the vision as long as you can. Practice intentionally visualizing the Cross as a way to develop your seeing skills.

2. Ask the Lord to bring an encouraging song to your mind. Note what you hear and pray for its meaning. When you lie down at night, ask Him to speak a scripture to you. When you wake up, ask Him for a song or a scripture that applies to your day or the challenge you are facing. Make a note of what you hear and pray about how to apply it.

3. Ask the Lord to make you more aware of how you feel around people. Ask Him to separate the emotions that belong to you from the emotions of other people. Reflect on a recent emotional reaction such as anxiety in a public place. Ask the Holy Spirit if the emotion belongs to you or to someone else.

4. The next time you feel something off about a person or place, lean into the feeling, asking the Lord to reveal what is hidden.

5. Ask the Lord to help you feel His presence, the presence of angels, and the atmosphere of heaven.

6. Psalm 34:8 encourages us to *"Taste and see that the Lord is good."* Ask the Lord if it is possible to actually taste His goodness. Ask Him to allow you to experience the tastes and smells of heaven here on the earth.

CHAPTER 3

WHEN AN ELEPHANT IS NOT AN ELEPHANT

I HAD JUST BEGUN MY TRAINING as a minister of inner healing. I was studying with *Elijah House* and had taken a course from Dr. Charles Kraft about prenatal healing. I was certainly no expert at the time I was asked to pray with a little girl who was in foster care. The child was friendly and willing to pray with me. She was very interested in God and learning more about His love for her. When I asked her to remember what being born had been like, she closed her eyes, looked, then opened her eyes and said with a giggle, "I look like a doll. A pink doll. Not like a real baby at all."

To this day, I believe she saw an accurate picture of how she felt at the time of her birth.

Because this happened at the beginning of my ministry, I had not yet learned how the Lord reveals truth through symbols, metaphors, and similes. The little girl, unwanted by her birth family, had entered the foster care system as an infant. She was later adopted by a loving family after her time in foster care. In the vision of her birth, she saw herself as unreal. If I knew then what I know now, I would have recognized that the picture of herself as a doll symbolized how she felt about being unwanted and how she was coping with it by imagining herself as an object without feelings. Just a doll. Not a real baby.

My point is this: Sensing spiritual realities is not difficult once you learn that it is possible and desirable. The difficulty lies in interpreting what you are discerning and then applying that understanding. So, let's start this chapter with a prayer.

> *Lord God, please give me ears to hear, eyes to see, and a heart that understands. You instruct me in Proverbs 4:5 to acquire wisdom and understanding. So I come to You, asking in the name of Jesus that You hold me back from jumping to conclusions. Please teach me to always turn to You for interpretation and application. Amen.*

Remember my story about smelling baby powder as I searched for mother cat's hidden kittens? The Holy Spirit used the scent of baby powder to lead me to her hiding place. The smell of baby powder makes me think of babies, so I simply followed the scent. My interpretation of the spiritual reality I was experiencing proved to be correct when I found the kittens.

We are rarely meant to understand spiritual experiences literally. What you sense within the realm of the spirit will mostly be symbolic, requiring interpretation. Occasionally, what you see, hear, and feel may be understood as the actual thing; that is, the rock you see is a rock and does not stand for anything else. For example, I was very worried that one of my cats would never use the very expensive pet door we had installed to give them access to our screened-in deck. I wondered if we had wasted our money. Then I had a dream. In the dream, my little cat was gleefully jumping through the pet door. A few weeks later, she did begin using the door. The dream was meant to be understood literally. God was telling me to calm down, all would be well. But it is rare that objects or people in our visions and dreams are meant to be understood literally.

Here is an example of a significant person in my life being used by God as a symbol. My stepdaughter Deborah is a professional actress. When she first began showing up in my dreams, I thought I was dreaming about her and for her. That kind of dream or vision does happen, but it is rare. I eventually realized that whenever Deborah shows up in my dreams, it means that I am concerned about my performance. Because she is a performer, who is naturally concerned about her performance since it is her livelihood, she makes an excellent symbol for performing or being concerned about performance. My point is this: keep in mind that the rock you see probably represents something else, and the significant person showing up in your visions and dreams most likely symbolizes something else. And the meaning of that depends upon what a rock means to you and what that person means to you.

A Quick Explanation of Symbols, Metaphors, and Similes

Symbols

Let's begin with symbols. A symbol is one thing that stands for or represents something else. For example, the American flag represents America. The flag is not America. It represents America. In my culture, a *white dove* represents *peace*. Wedding dresses are traditionally white because white also represents *purity*. But in Indian weddings, the bride often wears *red* which in that culture symbolizes *fertility, success,* and *marital bliss.* Red means *stop* and *danger* in my culture, and it means *success* and *bliss* in another culture. God often speaks through symbols and He expects you to understand those symbols according to what they mean in your life.

Here are a few symbols that Jesus used to describe Himself: the *Bread of Life* and the *Light of the World*. What do these symbols mean? Jesus is not actually a loaf of bread or a lamp on a table. Let's think together. What does *bread* mean — or even better — what did bread mean to those Jesus was talking to? Bread would have been the staple food that sustained life. When He called Himself the Bread of Life, He was also comparing Himself to the manna that sustained the life of Israel in the wilderness. His audience would have understood that Jesus was claiming to be the source of life, both for them and for their ancestors who had wandered in the wilderness. Jesus used bread to explain that He is our provider. By Him do we live.

> *"Your fathers ate the manna in the wilderness, and they died. This is the bread that comes down out of heaven, so that anyone may eat from it and not die. I am the living bread that came down out of heaven; if anyone eats from this bread, he will live forever; and the bread which I will give for the life of the world also is My flesh."*
>
> John 6:49–51

The word *light* is often used symbolically. Light can represent having a good idea or coming to an understanding. In scripture, light is a powerful symbol. The world was created with the words, *"Let there be light."* Think about that. Jesus described Himself as the *Light of the World*. He not only brings wisdom and understanding, He is declaring that as the Word of God, He created the world (Genesis 1:3 & John 1:1–4).

> *Then Jesus again spoke to them, saying, "I am the Light of the World; the one who follows Me will not walk in the darkness, but will have the Light of life."*
>
> John 8:12

Metaphors

Metaphors describe by comparing two things that are not like each other. For example, the saying that life is a journey compares life to a trip. The expression that there is an elephant in the room compares an uncomfortable issue that everyone is aware of — but no one wants to talk about — to a very large land mammal occupying human living space. Butterflies in the tummy compares the nervous feeling one gets before speaking in public or taking a test to the flutter of winged insects. The day spent on the couch binging television may earn you the title of couch potato. You are not a potato! But I know if I spend too much time on the couch, I kind of do feel like a potato.

Metaphors are such a part of our everyday language that we understand them without question. The Bible also uses metaphors. Read Isaiah 64:8 and see if you recognize the metaphor.

> *We are the clay, and You our potter ...*

The people are being compared to clay on a potter's wheel. The Lord is being compared to a potter who shapes the clay as He wills. What meaning are we meant to take away from this metaphor?

How about this one? Jesus calls Himself the *Good Shepherd* and us His sheep. As far as we know, Jesus never herded sheep and people are not sheep, so we know that He is using metaphorical language. What do you think He is trying to get us to understand by comparing Himself to a shepherd?

Similes

Like metaphors, similes compare one thing to another. The only difference is similes use the words *like* or *as* which makes it obvious that a comparison is being made. For example, *she is as busy as a bee*. Do you see a woman bustling about from chore to chore? *He is as stubborn as a mule.* How about this one? *After a hard day at work, he slept like a log.*

Here is a simile from Psalm 42:1, *"As the deer pants for the water brooks, so my soul pants for You, God."* Can you see the thirsty deer panting desperately for water? Isn't that an accurate way to describe our longing for God, especially during the hard times?

Jesus used similes in His teachings:

> *"Again, the kingdom of heaven is like a merchant seeking fine pearls."*
>
> Matthew 13:45

Trying to describe the kingdom of heaven must have been difficult because our human understanding is limited to what we have experienced in our lives. Here is another one. He presented another parable to them, saying:

> *"The kingdom of heaven is like a mustard seed, which a person took and sowed in his field."*
>
> Matthew 13:31

Notice that the Lord always used pictures and stories that His audience could relate to. When you engage in the spiritual realm, expect to see and sense the things that relate to your life experiences. Remember the story of the turnip plant? Even though our interpretation made sense, what Sam and I thought was incorrect. The recipient of that word of encouragement understood that turnip plant to represent a good and nutritious food. That the vision was of a turnip was particularly appropriate, because she does not like eating turnips. But she recognized that they were good for her. In the same way, she did not like that she was having to move, but she knew that the move was good for her. That the turnip was a green and healthy plant helped her embrace the challenges of making a move to a farm.

Scripture often uses symbolism, metaphor, and simile. As you cleanse and restore your generational line, expect to encounter this way of communicating. It is essential that we invite the Holy Spirit to provide the correct interpretation and application as we engage with spiritual realities. Keep in mind that the meaning behind symbols, metaphors, and similes will vary depending upon the person.

But What if the Elephant IS an Elephant?

Just to make things interesting, there are times when spiritual realities are a combination of symbols and realism. And very occasionally, you may experience a spiritual reality that is meant to be understood as completely literal, no interpretation needed. For example, the angels that appeared in the dreams of Joseph who was betrothed to Mary were literal angels delivering literal messages to him. The angel that led Peter out of prison was an actual angel and Peter's escape was happening in real time. Peter thought he was in a vision.

> *And the angel said to him, "Put on your belt and strap on your sandals." And he did so. And he said to him, "Wrap your cloak around you and follow me." And he went out and continued to follow, and yet he did not know that what was being done by the angel was real, but thought he was seeing a vision.*
>
> Acts 12:8–9

When my husband Sam was facing hernia surgery, he felt very anxious. He had undergone two other surgeries that resulted in prolonged and painful recoveries, so he was understandably nervous about this one. As he lay in bed the night before, he had a reoccurring vision of a utility knife slicing into his belly. This vision was putting a picture to his fear. Dreams will do this too. When he finally fell asleep, he had a dream that he was at a family celebration. The family was not his biological family, but he knew that they were family. He felt exhilarated. The following morning very early, he arose and went for a walk. As he was walking, he experienced an opened-eye vision. He saw himself on the operating table. The surgeon and staff were gathered at the end of the table getting ready to start, when a brightly lit Jesus appeared in the midst of them, and Sam heard, "This is a very special patient."

The utility knife was symbolic of Sam's fear. The dream of the family party was symbolical, but of what Sam did not know until later. The opened-eye vision was not symbolic at all. It was a realistic picture of God's involvement with Sam's upcoming surgery.

Prior to being wheeled into surgery, his doctor approached Sam asking if he could pray. He explained that he prayed for all his patients before operating. Sam was thrilled to accept. The surgeon laid hands on him and prayed that Jesus would guide him as he operated. I joined Sam after he was recovering in his room. His nurse had a small tattoo on her wrist. I asked her the meaning and she said it was a scripture verse to remind her that she was serving God as she cared for her patients. Later Sam learned that his anesthesiologist was a devoted Christian, as were many of the staff employed at that surgery center. Sam's family was with him as the dream had revealed. On his follow-up visit to the doctor, Sam recounted his vision. The doctor told him that in his office, he had a painting of Jesus guiding the hands of a surgeon.

What To Keep In Mind

Why are some spiritual experiences literal while most others are symbolic? I do not know for sure. This interesting scripture tells us that we see spiritual realities as if we are looking into a poorly lighted mirror. Have you ever tried looking into a mirror when the room is dark? You should try it.

> *For now we see in a mirror dimly, but then face to face; now I know in part, but then I will know fully, just as I also have been fully known.*
>
> 1 Corinthians 13:12

The fact is this: We are utterly dependent upon the Holy Spirit to show us by word of knowledge, wisdom, and discernment of spirits what happened so many years ago to our people. It is only under His guidance that we can arrive at any understanding of what our people decided to believe about themselves, others, and life. Once we know what is hidden within the heart of our tribe, we can begin the work of restoring and releasing the goodness woven into our design.

Let's pray:

> *Dear Lord, You are the Maker of heaven and earth, and the Maker of all the mysteries that are mine to search out. Job 12:22 states that You "reveal mysteries from the darkness, and bring the deep darkness into light." Joseph of the coat-of-many-colors teaches me that all interpretation belongs to You (Genesis 40:8). As I seek to restore my generational line, I ask You to guide me. Interpret what I see and hear. Help me recognize the symbols, metaphors, and similes that You use to speak. Bring Your understanding so that I can successfully release all the goodness that You have poured into my people.*
>
> *In Jesus' name, I ask this of You. Amen.*

Practice

1. Psalm 23 is one long metaphor. As you read through the Psalm, pick out the symbols and comparisons. Consider what the psalmist meant by comparing God to a shepherd. What do you think the green pastures, quiet waters, and the rod and staff represent?

2. Reflect on a recent dream or vision. List its symbols and ask the Holy Spirit what they represent.

3. While Joseph was in prison, he interpreted two dreams. (See Genesis 40). Both dreams contain symbols unique to the dreamers. Read Genesis 40 and think about the symbols used for the cupbearer and for the baker. Why do you think the symbols in their dreams were different?

4. Set aside 15 minutes to pray, "Holy Spirit, show me one spiritual reality related to my tribe's heart beliefs." Note any vision, sound, or emotion that arises. For each, ask, "Is this literal (like Joseph's angelic dreams) or symbolic (like Pharaoh's dreams)? What does it mean?" Journal your interpretation and pray John 16:13, asking for clarity. Repeat this practice weekly, noting how your discernment grows.

CHAPTER 4

THE HEART IS A BOSS

If our hearts condemn us, we know that God is greater than our hearts ...

1 John 3:20 NIV

FOR THOSE OF YOU WHO have read *The Quiet Heart* and *The Performing Heart*, this chapter will be a refresher. If you have not yet read the other *Heart* books, please pay close attention to this discussion about the human heart. Understanding the role of the heart and its functions are essential to completing an effective generational restoration.

Let me clarify that the following discussion is NOT about the heart as a symbol or a metaphor. When I use the word heart, I am NOT talking about emotions or love or the center of things. I am NOT talking about your spirit, soul, or mind. I am talking about your actual physical heart. You may be wondering what your actual physical heart has to do with restoring your generational line. Let me explain the importance of your individual heart and then I will explain how this applies to your tribal heart.

The Heart

As in water a face reflects the face, so the heart of a person reflects the person.

Proverbs 27:19

The Bible uses the Hebrew word 'lēb' for *heart* and the Greek word 'kardia' for *heart*. Both of these words mean the physical heart and together add up to over one thousand mentions in scripture. If we believe the Bible, rather than claims that *heart* does not refer to the physical heart, we must ask ourselves why there is so much emphasis on the physical heart. Just as an aside, the Bible does not mention the brain at all, yet we have no problem believing that our physical brains are important or that they perform the marvelous and mystifying functions called thinking and remembering. According to the Bible and cardiovascular researchers, our physical hearts are also capable of thinking and remembering.

The following is an excerpt from *The Performing Heart*.

> A branch of science called neurocardiology has found evidence that the human heart (the physical organ) has its own way of thinking and feeling. Their studies suggest that the thoughts and feelings of your heart exert tremendous and measurable control over how you interpret life's experiences.[4] These scientists also believe that your heart takes your early life experiences and, from them, teaches you what to expect from life.[5] Essentially, these experts are coming to the conclusion that the human heart — the pump in the chest — has a mind of its own.

---

4   Rollin McCraty, *Science of the Heart: Exploring the Role of the Heart in Human Performance, Volume 2* (Boulder Creek, California, HeartMath Institute, 2015), 1-2.

5   McCraty, Mike Atkinson and Dana Tomasino, *Science of the Heart: Exploring the Role of the Heart in Human Performance,* Publication No. 01-001, (Boulder Creek, California, HeartMath Institute, 2001), 8.

This means that your heart uses your early life experiences to create a belief system for you. This belief system begins to build while you are in the womb — *at which time you receive your generational download* — and during your earliest childhood experiences. This belief system is stored within the physical heart.⁶

Your Personal Heart Belief System

As Jesus pointed out in Luke 6:45, your heart stores your belief system. This belief system was constructed when you were a child as you reacted to your early life circumstances, beginning during your time in the womb. As you reacted to your environment and the important people in your life, you developed beliefs about yourself, relationships, and life. Please recall from Chapter 2 the three most significant beliefs that are hidden within a tribal heart.

Let's go over them again.

1. Identity — who we are as a people.
2. Relationships — how others perceive us and will treat us.
3. Life — this is the way life will treat us as a people.

As an individual, you also have beliefs about these three significant things.

1. Who you are as a person. This is your identity.
2. How others see you and how they will treat you. This is your relationships.
3. How life will treat you. This is your perception of reality.

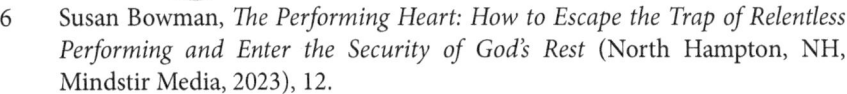

---

6 Susan Bowman, *The Performing Heart: How to Escape the Trap of Relentless Performing and Enter the Security of God's Rest* (North Hampton, NH, Mindstir Media, 2023), 12.

Because of the fall, the world is a chaotic place, filled with people behaving badly. As we experience this confusion and chaos, we develop beliefs that are very painful. Because these childhood beliefs are painful and confusing, we do what children do — we blame ourselves and we hide from what we believe. Proverbs 4:23 teaches us that all of life is filtered through this hidden heart belief system developed when we were too small to know better.

The Three Components of a Personal Heart Belief System

1. Your identity — Who you believe you are.
2. Relationships — How you believe important people will behave. This is based upon the actions of your father and mother.
3. Life — How life will treat you.

Proverbs 4:23 states that all of life flows through the heart. Because the heart stores your belief system, and because that belief system is mostly hidden from your conscious awareness, you will be unaware that all of your experiences and perceptions are being filtered through this childhood set of beliefs.

Here is an example. If your father was absent, then your heart will store the belief that the important man will not be there for you. Because this belief is painful, it will be hidden behind vows to never remember it. Nonetheless, even hidden, such a belief filters all of your important relationships with men. You will feel it as the expectation that the man will not be there for you. This feeling and fear of abandonment will intensify in times of stress.

Now let's apply this to the corporate heart of your tribe. The corporate heart stores the tribe's belief system because, at some point in the past, everyone agreed that what they believe is always true for them. Notice the word *always*. Unlike the beliefs of the mind, heart beliefs are pretty much set in stone. They can be changed, but changing them requires intentional intervention. *The Quiet Heart, The Performing Heart,* and the YouTube series *Your Identity and The Heart* teach how to recognize heart level beliefs and how to change them.

The tribe's agreed-upon set of beliefs is downloaded into the following generations and stored within each individual heart. This download of beliefs strongly influences how and what you believe about yourself, relationships, and life.

The Tribal Heart Belief System

Now let's apply what you have learned about your individual heart belief system to a tribal heart belief system.

Your responses to your early life experiences resulted in your personal belief system. What you believe about who you are; what you believe about how people will treat you, and what you believe about how life works for you is hidden within your heart.

Your tribe also responded to its early life circumstances. How it, as a people group, reacted to trauma, diseases, lack, loss, disappointment, and dishonor shaped how it perceived itself. As the tribe attempted to navigate the many challenges encountered in the hostile environment we call the fall, a common belief system was being built and stored within the hearts of each individual tribe member. This is a collective or shared group belief system. This system includes what the tribe believes about who they are; what they believe about how people will treat them, and what they believe about how life works for them as a group who shares the same identity. This tribal belief system merges with the individual heart beliefs of each person belonging to the tribe. Here is a metaphor for you. Think of your heart as a pitcher. Think of your beliefs as the water filling that pitcher. Now, visualize a packet of Kool-Aid being stirred into the water. The Kool-Aid flavors the entire pitcher of water. In the same way, the shared beliefs of your tribe flavors your personal heart belief system.

The Three Components of a Tribal Heart Belief System

1. A group identity — Who we believe we are as a people.
2. Relationships with others within and outside of our tribe — How important and powerful people see us and treat us a people group. This includes God.
3. Life — What we can expect from life.

As you work with the Holy Spirit to restore your bloodline, the most important thing to uncover are the beliefs stored within the tribal heart. Look carefully for the tribe's (shared) heart-level beliefs, because the beliefs the tribe has stored within its heart not only strongly influence what you accept as true, they control identity, relationships, and the course of life.

Here is an example. If your tribe believes that no matter how hard they work, they can never get ahead because the odds are always unfairly stacked against them, then you will be strongly influenced to believe that you can never get ahead because you are always treated unfairly. This belief about success and failure will continue to be passed down to subsequent generations until it is located, removed, and replaced with God's plan for your tribe.

The tribal heart belief system is constructed from shared experiences. What the actual experiences are is not as important as the beliefs that emerged as the tribe responded to painful and traumatic events. *It is the beliefs stored within the heart that determine the outcome for you as an individual and for your tribe.* If what the tribe believes about itself, relationships, and life is painful, it will hide what it believes behind all manner of vows taken to escape and manage pain. It is these vows that hide what the tribe believes. This causes the beliefs stored within the tribal heart to be passed on to the next generation without any context for why they believe what they believe.

The Functions of the Physical Heart

According to scripture the physical heart performs many important functions. It also behaves in unique ways. We will look at those behaviors in the next chapter. Let's take a few moments and consider what the Bible teaches us about the functions of the heart.

Functions of the Physical Heart

1. The heart *feels* (Psalm 143:4).
2. The heart *determines the outcome of our lives* (Proverbs 4:23).
3. The heart *reflects who we really are* (Proverbs 27:19).
4. *The enemy targets* the heart (Psalm 64:6).
5. The heart functions as a *storehouse* (Luke 6:45).
6. *We can take dominion* over our hearts (John 14:1).
7. *We believe* with the heart (Romans 10:10). And, what the heart believes is hidden (1 Peter 3:4).

As you can see, our hearts are extremely important, and it is essential to our well-being and our witness that we become experts at discerning our heart belief system (both individual and tribal) and skilled at bringing healing and freedom by reprogramming our hearts to believe truth.

Let's pray:

> *Dearest Lord, You created the human heart so that it functions as the storehouse of my belief system. Because of the fall, my heart and the tribal heart of my people have stored wrong beliefs. Please guide me as I search my bloodline for the beliefs stored within it. Help me uncover any hidden beliefs that dishonor You and hurt my people. Help me replace these wrong beliefs with truth. Root and ground my heart and my tribal heart in Your grace and love. Amen.*

Guard your heart above all else, for it determines the course of your life.

Proverbs 4:23 NLT

Practice

1. Discuss the heart's biblical role with a mentor or trusted person, explaining its importance as a storehouse of belief. Note their feedback.

2. Ask the Lord to reveal to you one component of your inherited tribal belief system. Listen for language that describes what is believed about identity, relationships, and life. Then ask the Lord to show you a component of your personal belief system that agrees with the inherited beliefs of your people. Do not worry about doing anything with this information. We will discuss that later.

3. Reflect on a painful personal belief such as I am unlovable. Ask the Holy Spirit if it is influenced by a tribal belief and pray for clarity.

4. Pray the chapter's closing prayer, asking God to reveal one tribal heart belief about identity, relationships, or life. Note any emotions or impressions.

5. Read Proverbs 27:19 and Luke 6:45. Pray for dominion over your heart (John 14:27), asking God to align it with His truth.

CHAPTER 5

YOU ARE WHAT YOUR HEART BELIEVES

I want to take another chapter to further emphasize the importance of learning to access both your personal and tribal heart belief systems. Proverbs 4:23 instructs us to *"guard your heart above all else."* The words *"above all else"* make this instruction extremely significant. The proverb reveals that ALL of life flows through your 'lēb', that is your physical heart. Much time has passed since Proverbs was written and our understanding of how the heart functions has become muddied. Only recently as cardiovascular researchers have conducted extensive studies on the physical heart has our understanding begun to return to what the ancient people of the Bible knew about the human heart.

Here is what Dr. J. Andrew Armour, one of the early pioneers in neurocardiology, says about the physical heart. He writes that the heart's "elaborate circuitry enables it to act independently of the cranial brain — to learn, remember, and even feel and sense."[7] He explains that during early life a child's heart responds to a chaotic environment by generating a measurable disordered rhythm pattern. Disharmony is stored as normal or as "the way life works for me" within the heart. The heart then teaches the brain to expect disharmony in life.[8]

What you believe within your heart is established during childhood. If childhood was painful, chaotic, and uncertain, the heart will store the belief that life will ALWAYS be painful, chaotic, and uncertain. Then all your experiences are filtered through this heart belief. What the heart believes exerts so much influence over your life that it will compel you to create chaos and uncertainty where there is none or compel you to *see and feel* chaos, pain, and uncertainty where there is none. What you believe within your heart will inject disharmony into every harmonious situation.

Now let's apply that to the tribal heart. Recall the example from the previous chapter. A tribe accepted at the heart level that they would always be treated unfairly. This is a tribal heart belief that resulted from some unfortunate experience that happened many, many years ago. The descendants of this tribe inherit the belief, and because the heart guides how reality is perceived, they automatically believe that they are always treated unfairly. They will be compelled to view life through the distorted lens of that belief.

This is why Proverbs 4:23 warns us to guard our hearts above all else. What we believe within our hearts determines the course of our lives. This is also why I focus generational restoration on discovering the tribal heart beliefs. Once the tribal heart beliefs are resolved, other common issues affecting your generational inheritance are much more easily and more effectively remedied.

---

7   McCraty, *Science of the Heart*, Publication No. 01-001, 4.
8   McCraty, *Science of the Heart*, Publication No. 01-001, 8.

The Heart Informs the Brain (not the other way around)

I was taught to renew my mind by replacing unhappy thoughts with scripture. Perhaps you were also taught to override pain-filled thinking and feelings by choosing to believe the things we are supposed to believe. For example, when you feel afraid, you may try to concentrate your thoughts on a verse like:

> *He has not given us a spirit of fear.*
>
> 2 Timothy 1:7 NKJV

Have you tried doing this? Did it slow down that clippety-cloppety heart rate? No?

Focusing on scripture or worship is not a bad coping mechanism. I have used it many times, but it does not address the underlying heart beliefs that trap us in a fear response. This is because once the heart is settled into what it believes, it will continue to inform the brain about what to expect. We carry these expectations into all of our significant relationships. When circumstances occur that resemble early childhood experiences, your heart remembers what you believe and organizes its heartbeat around those beliefs. Clippety-clop. These disordered heartbeats then inform your brain, and the rest of your body, about what you can expect based upon your early experiences.

Dr. Armour's research validates scripture that emphasizes the importance of the heart over the brain. What is hidden within the heart informs the brain. The brain does not inform the heart.

> *For it is with your heart that you believe ...*
>
> Romans 10:10 NIV

Tribal Heart Beliefs are Influencers

Tribal heart beliefs exert the same influence over you as personal heart beliefs. As a matter of fact, your personal heart beliefs will align with the tribal beliefs that you inherit. Let's say that you are treated unfairly at school. Someone breaks into the line ahead of you. If you have inherited the tribal heart belief that you will always be treated unfairly, such rude behavior will have quite a punch to it. Whereas, if your tribe does not have that belief about unfairness influencing how it perceives the behaviors of others, you might be annoyed. You might complain. But you will not be thrown into a mysterious despair or boil over with anger. There will not be this overwhelming sense that this is what *always happens* to you.

Unique Behaviors of the Heart

As in water face reflects face, So the heart of man reflects man.

Proverbs 27:19

Because this book is meant to help you restore your generational line, I want to focus on certain behaviors of the heart so that you can recognize when you are running into a heart belief. Like your mind, your heart is capable of expressing what it believes through emotions and thoughts. Unlike your mind, which is capable of feeling emotions appropriate to the present situation, the heart expresses the emotions we felt as children. Your mind is capable of thinking broadly over a wide range of topics. It is capable of considering the gray areas of a complicated matter. Your heart thinks in the patterns laid down when you were a child. It thinks in the patterns you inherited from your tribe. This means that the heart is rigid in how it thinks.

Here is a metaphor for you. Imagine your heart is the engine of a train. The cars it pulls are composed of the rest of your body, including your brain. The engine of our imaginary train runs along a track laid down in previous times by your ancestors. The track determines the direction of the train. If you want the train to go in another direction, you must change the track. It is the same for your heart. If you want your heart to travel toward God, you must change the belief system stored within it. Here is another metaphor for you. Think of your heart as a very inflexible, rule-loving, behind-the-scenes, stuck-in-the-mud manager. How great-grandma did the thing is how the thing will be done. Do not ask questions! If you want to change the rules so that you may grow into an honest and cheerful relationship with God, you must fire the old manager and clean out his office.

1. The heart thinks in patterns.

As Dr. Armour points out, the heart records your childhood experiences as a framework into which all subsequent experiences are fitted. For example, if your mother was cold and critical, your heart will form a belief such as this: *All important women are always cold and critical.* This becomes the track controlling how you perceive all interactions with important women. Until a better track is intentionally built, the heart will insist that how mother treated you is how other significant women will treat you.

This applies to the beliefs hidden within the tribal heart as well. Until a better track is intentionally built into your tribal heart, you will be compelled to view life through the filter of ancient tribal beliefs.

2. The heart stores the emotions you felt at the time you believed something significant.

The shame felt when mother rejects you or father abuses you is stored within the heart along with what you believe. Whenever someone's behavior resembles your painful childhood experiences, your heart will remember the pain and release the emotions it stores. This flood of unresolved emotion may feel overwhelming because it arrives without any explanation or context. This causes confusion. The mind will insist that whatever is happening in the present moment is the cause of your feelings, but remember that your heart releases what you believe along with the emotions whenever an event happens that is even close to an important early life experience. To put it in a nutshell, unresolved emotion is stored in the heart and surfaces when faced with a situation similar to the original childhood experience. So how does that apply to the tribal heart?

Strong emotions in times of distress are often unresolved. When those emotions are shared within a tribe, they are stored within the tribal heart. For example, the tribe that believes it is always treated unfairly will have collected a lot of despair, frustration, and anger. This emotional state is shared among the tribe members as part of what they believe. As children join the tribe, they are downloaded with both the beliefs and the emotions held by the tribe.

As you conduct your generational restoration, you may experience a flood of inexplicable emotions. Confusion is the natural result. Do not be discouraged. Confusion is an uncomfortable but encouraging sign that you have tapped into the tribal heart. I will discuss strategies on managing these historical emotions in another chapter. On a positive note, the love and acceptance you felt as a child, if offered on a consistent basis, are also stored within the heart.

3. *The heart speaks in absolutes.*

When you connect with heart beliefs, both personal and tribal, you will notice two things. First, the belief feels unshakeable. Second, the language that expresses these kinds of beliefs usually contains absolute words such as ALWAYS and NEVER; NO ONE and EVERYONE. This is how the heart believes. These words signal that you have tapped into the tribal heart.

Let's look again at the tribe that believes it will always be treated unfairly. Notice that the tribe believes that it will ALWAYS be treated unfairly. The *always* informs us that we have uncovered a tribal heart belief.

4. **The heart believes absolutely.**

Not only does the heart think and speak in absolutes, it believes absolutely. This is the reason why heart beliefs feel so true. We may be able to get along in life reasonably well, but let something happen that resembles our unresolved childhood or tribal experiences and what we *really* believe will surface with a vengeance.

You may be asking why it is important for you to understand how the heart behaves. When you are conducting a generational restoration, you will encounter lots of distractions. Please keep in mind that what matters the most is not what happened to your people. What matters is what they believe about what happened. In order to locate what your tribe believes; you must unlock the heart. If you do not understand how the heart functions, you will miss the most important thing.

At the beginning of this section, I referenced Proverbs 27:19. Let's look at that again, reading it this way.

As in water face reflects face, so the heart of [the tribe] reflects [the tribe].

A Heart-Focused Generational Restoration

You may be familiar with other approaches to generational cleansing. In my experience, these models do not focus on discovering and repairing the beliefs stored within the tribal heart. Instead, they focus on sin, trauma, and damage done by the enemy.

John Sandford, founder of *Elijah House* and apostle of the inner healing movement, taught a principle called 'fruit to root'. Sin responses to trauma are the *fruit* of what we believe. Generational patterns of sin such as addictions, abuse, chronic failures, broken relationships, mental illnesses, and self-hatred are examples of *fruit*. Demonic access to a tribe's bloodline is *fruit*. Such access is granted because of something the tribe believed.

Sandford warns that you cannot kill a tree by picking the fruit. You must destroy the *root*. The beliefs hidden within the tribal heart are the *roots*.

Let's take a moment and apply this to the widespread practice of Freemasonry. Almost all of us have some version of Freemasonry in our background and Christian deliverance has developed a protocol for removing the covenants, vows, and curses that accompany it. So why are people who have been through the renunciations not experiencing lasting freedom? I have been through those lengthy renunciations three or four times myself, and I think it is good to renounce all association with Freemasonry, but we must go one step further and ask this question: Why did my people become involved in that cult in the first place? What did they *believe* that made Freemasonry attractive to them?

What I have found after conducting hundreds of generational restorations is the promises of honor, acceptance, and safety are what make Freemasonry and other cults appealing. When a tribe believes that it is a weak people who have been abandoned by God and are at risk from its environment and/or its neighbors, it is vulnerable to being seduced by the promises of Freemasonry. It is this foundational belief that controls how the tribe perceives reality. It sees itself as weak and alone. It sees others as potential threats. It sees life as dangerous. No wonder the tribe was attracted to the promises of protection, belonging, and prestige offered by Freemasonry. What the tribe believes is the root of the problem and must be addressed if you and your people are going to enjoy sustainable healing and freedom.

As we continue, I will teach you practical ways to recognize and access your tribal heart belief system. Once you know what your tribe believes, you can dismantle the fear-based heart belief system that you inherited and, under the guidance of the Holy Spirit, rebuild a belief system that releases into the earth the abundant goodness that the Lord has placed within your bloodline.

Let's pray:

> *Dear God, Creator of heaven and earth, the beliefs of the heart are mostly hidden. If I am to discover them so that I can address what we believe at the deepest level, I will need You to guide me. Only You can set me free. I lean on You alone. Please guide me and give me Your wisdom and courage to address the beliefs within my tribal heart and those within my personal heart. Please take away any pain so that this work is bearable.*
>
> *In Jesus' name I ask this of You. Amen.*

Surely He took up our pain and bore our suffering,

Isaiah 53:4 NIV

Practice

1. Consider your important relationships with either the man or woman. How do your current relationships mirror your relationship with your father or mother?

2. Have you ever tried to "think" your way out of a strong emotion such as fear, shame, or sadness using scripture or positive thoughts? What was the result? How might focusing on your heart's beliefs change your approach to this struggle?

3. Consider a belief or emotional pattern that seems to run in your family (e.g., distrust, perfectionism, victimhood). How does this pattern show up in your behavior or expectations? What might this reveal about your tribal heart beliefs?

4. Over the next week, keep a journal of moments when you feel a strong emotional reaction such as anger, despair, or fear. For each instance, write down the situation that triggered the emotion, the emotion itself and its intensity, any thoughts that contain absolute words like *always, never,* and *everyone*. Then ask the Lord to remind you of a childhood or family experience this reaction might connect to.

    At the end of the week, review your entries. Look for patterns that might point to a heart belief, for example *I am always overlooked* or *No one can be trusted*. Pray for discernment about whether this belief is personal, tribal, or both.

5. When you experience a flood of intense negative emotion, pause and pray immediately. Use this prayer as a guide:

   Lord Jesus, this emotion feels overwhelming. I believe it is connected to a belief in my heart. Please show me what my heart believes and heal the root of this pain. Replace this belief with Your truth.

   Write down any impressions or memories that surface. Over time, track how this practice affects your emotional responses.

CHAPTER 6

STARTING POINT

They said, "Come, let us build for ourselves a city, and a tower whose top will reach into heaven, and let us make for ourselves a name, otherwise we will be scattered abroad over the face of all the earth."

Genesis 11:4

MANY YEARS AGO, I ATTENDED a seminar promising to introduce the concept of generational cleansing and to give some opportunities to put into practice what we learned. The learning part went okay, although there were more questions than answers, but the *put-into-practice* part was a huge mess. I had already been introduced to generational restoration by the late Dr. Tom Hawkins. He was kind enough to explain the principles, and Arthur Burk had arranged for a colleague to walk me through a personal cleanse.

But for most who attended the seminar the idea that ancestral actions had the power to affect them personally was very new. While the attendees were still mulling over the implications, or whether they even agreed that the actions of generations past were anything to be concerned about — after all, we are new creatures in Christ — we were instructed to gather in groups, choose a person, and begin a cleanse for that person.

One thing I found interesting, as I watched the efforts of each team disintegrate into confusion and ultimately chaos, was how the lack of structure became the center of conflict. We had been told to begin the cleanse by asking the Lord to reveal how many years ago the problem, whatever the problem was, had started and where had it started, as in what country. As you can imagine, everyone on the team heard something different to the eventual exasperation of the randomly selected, untrained team leader. Another interesting problem surfaced as different team members had different ideas about what sin was bad enough to result in generational problems. Opinions varied widely, depending on each person's personal experience. So, the "cleanse" devolved into arguments and confusion. People left the seminar unsettled and upset.

Since that time, I have conducted hundreds of generational restorations. As I practiced, I tried different models and strategies, discarding most and finally coming to the realization that sin is the result of what the tribe believes, as is demonic intrusion.

Eve is the first example of this pattern. She believed what the enemy told her, which caused her to believe that God had withheld something extraordinarily desirable from her. This belief led her to be willing to do *whatever it takes* to get what she believed she lacked. Adam believed that he had to choose between God and his beloved. He was willing to do *whatever it takes* to keep his wife. Their sin, ALL sin, grows out of wrong beliefs. My point is this: Look first for the beliefs hidden within the tribal heart. The where and the when those beliefs became a problem may be interesting but are not important.

As you begin to practice cleansing and restoring your generational line or those of others, please remember the chaos of my early experience. Here are my takeaways from that experience. We will call this section

What To Avoid

1. Team is too large:

Always keep your team small, three or four people, including the person receiving the cleanse. When you first begin, limit your team to people you trust and who agree with the process. As you gain experience you can take the time to train new people as the Lord leads. I do conduct generational cleanses one-on-one with success. But I really appreciate the advantages of working with a solid, unified team. The gifts and insights a good team brings are invaluable.

What do I do if I have no one to help me?

You can conduct a cleanse on yourself with just the guidance and help of the Holy Spirit. Most of my personal generational work has been just the Holy Spirit and myself. This means slowly chipping away at your tribal belief system instead of intense hours-long sessions with a team or with a minister. There are advantages to both. The experiences of a well-trained team or minister are very useful, but not always available. Working alone with the Holy Spirit builds your relationship with Him which is absolutely a benefit without price. Because this approach goes more slowly, you have time to process what you learn which is another very valuable benefit. Working rapidly with a team is more like chopping a path through dense jungle with a machete (notice the simile). Many fine details and how to apply what is discovered often fall by the wayside with a team approach.

If you are patient with the process and with yourself and willing to endure the confusion that is inevitable with or without a team, you can clean up and restore your bloodline without another human's help. It takes more time to uncover and understand what the Lord is revealing because you are learning the skills yourself and not leaning on others who are more experienced. But as you practice you will become better at understanding what the Lord shows you. Later chapters will explain what to do with what you are shown.

2. Literal interpretations:

Most of what you discern in the spiritual realm will need interpretation because most of it is symbolic. Recognize that each team member will be listening, looking, and sensing for words of knowledge, wisdom, and discernment of spirits. We only grow in accuracy and confidence as we practice. When there is disagreement or confusion, stop the cleanse and seek the Lord for clarity. If no clarity comes, back burner the confusion and move on. God will return you to it if and when it is necessary. Be kind to yourself and each other and, above all, keep practicing.

3. Focus is off:

Do not ask for specific times and places. You are working with a lost history that only the Lord understands with complete accuracy. Do not worry about the when or where. You are looking for the what: *What happened to the people? What is the important trauma or event?* And you are looking for the how: *How did the people respond to what happened?* That information will help you uncover what the tribe believed as it responded to the event.

4. No Structure:

Structure. Structure. Structure. Stay within a predetermined structure so that you do not become lost in the unknowns. I will describe the structure that I use when doing a deep and thorough cleanse.

The Tower of Babel

After these things I looked, and behold, a great multitude which no one could count, from every nation and all tribes, peoples, and languages, standing before the throne and before the Lamb, clothed in white robes ...

Revelation 7:9

There is no way to pinpoint the time in history when a tribe settled into its heart belief system. The one thing that I am certain of is that the tribe developed its belief system in ancient times. What you know about your family, even as far back as your great-grandparents, will only be an expression of the fruit resulting from beliefs hardened into place centuries ago.

So where do we begin our cleanse? Here is my approach and, so far, it has proven to be effective, especially in these two ways.

1. It stops the confusion of trying to hear when the cleanse should start.
2. It ensures that the cleanse begins *before* the event that prompted the tribe to make permanent decisions about its identity, relationships, and life. This helps to discover the tribe's gifting since we begin before it was overwhelmed by painful heart beliefs.

Consider with me the Tower of Babel which happened approximately 4300 years ago. Imagine what the people believed before they began building that tower. It is pretty obvious that they believed in unity. Genesis 11 records that the whole earth shared a common language and even the *"same words."* They were one great big tribe. Then they began building a city and tower so that they would not become *"scattered abroad over the face of the whole earth"* (Genesis 11:4). This agreement to congregate in one place violated God's command to *"Be fruitful and multiply, and fill the earth"* (Genesis 1:28). There was no "filling of the earth" going on. They were building in and up. Why?

Beyond sharing a common language, I believe that our ancestors shared a deep, fearful distrust of God. Recall that the builders of the Tower of Babel were directly descended from the handful of survivors of a cataclysmic, worldwide flood that destroyed all life. All life. Everything was gone. God completely recreated the earth. It would not take much to transfer blaming the consequences of the horrible sinfulness of mankind to blaming God.

> *Then the Lord saw that the wickedness of man was great on the earth, and that every intent of the thoughts of his heart was only evil continually.*
>
> Genesis 6:5

This is what I believe led to the decision to build a tower that reached into heaven. It was life insurance. At least some would survive a future flood. It was at that point that God intervened and redirected humanity by *scattering them abroad over the face of all the earth* (Genesis 11:8).

Now, there are two traumatic events that may be traced back to God engraved upon the heart of humanity: the cataclysmic re-creation of the earth and the sudden, and no doubt alarming, dividing of humanity into tribes.

As the people organized into tribes that shared the same language, they began wandering throughout the earth. Every tribe carried within it the traumas they had suffered, and every tribe was tempted to shift the blame for those traumas away from their choices and over to God.

As the tribes wandered, they encountered many challenges, including hardships of all kinds. As they responded to those challenges, a shared identity developed. They already carried within their tribal heart a set of beliefs about how God would treat them. As they encountered other tribes, beliefs about how they would be treated by others formed. Eventually, expectations about how life worked for the tribe became solidified.

You and I are the descendants of these people.

But That Is So Long Ago!

Yes. The Tower of Babel is many years back, but it is a very good place to start a generational restoration because your generational line did not begin with great-great-grandpa. Tribal heart beliefs are handed down from generation to generation, so it is best to begin the cleanse at the time that life-altering decisions were being made. I am not saying that the tribal belief system you inherited necessarily began at the Tower of Babel. But if you start there and come forward with your cleanse, you will not miss anything significant. Also, keep in mind that what is seen in the family line is the fruit of that fallen belief system. To get to the root you must get to the beginning. Starting at the Tower ensures that you do that.

Now in the next chapter, let's learn how to approach the Lord in order to begin your cleanse.

Practice

1. Discuss the two historic traumatic events with the Lord. Ask Him if you secretly blame Him for your personal suffering and the suffering of the world. Ask Him to help you redirect any blame you may have against Him to the correct source.

2. Recall a family story about a significant event such as Great-grandfather lost his business. Pray, "Holy Spirit, show me if a tribal heart belief surfaced when the trauma occurred. What was that belief?" Note any beliefs surfacing such as *We can never recover.* Compare the event and belief, asking, "How has this belief shaped my family's expectations about life?"

CHAPTER 7

MERCY, GRACE, AND WEIRDNESS ABOUND

Therefore let us draw near with confidence to the throne of grace, so that we may receive mercy and find grace to help in time of need.

Hebrews 4:16 ESV

Now that a starting point for a generational restoration has been established, let's learn how to begin the actual cleanse. Prayer comes first, of course, but the prayer I suggest you begin with is not your typical prayer. This prayer knocks on the door of the spiritual realm while making it safe to go through that door when it opens.

It is also designed to help you become aware of the spiritual realm. Although we are surrounded by and live within the spiritual realm, we are not always aware of it. One reason for this lack of awareness is because the natural realm is so compelling to our senses. And, also, we just lack training. With practice you will learn to tune into the spiritual realm and learn to notice when it is speaking to you. I want you to understand that I am not writing about a fantasy world that you created to escape a painful reality. God may use a self-created fantasy world to communicate with you, using the characters and settings you invented to reveal the truth. But the worlds created by unhappy children are escapism fantasy. The spiritual realm is real.

Here is the prayer that I begin with. Notice that it is a very simple and short prayer. Please modify as the Lord leads.

The Beginning Prayer

> *In the name of Jesus, I ask the Lord God to forbid the interference of all evil spirits and everything captured, controlled, and influenced by them. I ask the Lord to rebuke them so there will be no reporting, recording, observing, or eavesdropping. I ask Jesus to cancel any invitation — either generational or personal — they may have so they do not attend. I ask the Lord to direct His angels to remove any evil being that does not obey these orders and escort them to the place appointed for them.*
>
> *Lord God, Father and Creator, please make it safe to do this work. Please take the reins and guide us so that Your purposes are accomplished.*

Now, let's take that prayer apart.

1. "In the name of Jesus" is recognition that He is Savior, authority, righteousness — all that is necessary to gain access to the Father. It also identifies the one who is praying as His child.

2. "I ask the Lord God to forbid the interference of all evil spirits and everything captured, controlled, and influenced by them" identifies the forces that stand against this work being accomplished.

3. "There will be no reporting, recording, observing, or eavesdropping. I ask Jesus to cancel any invitation" informs them that any generational rights are revoked and they are not allowed to be present. It establishes a clear boundary.

4. "I ask the Lord to direct His angels to remove any evil being that does not obey these orders and escort them to the place appointed for them" is a request for angelic protection for yourself and the work you are doing.

5. "Lord God, Father and Creator, please make it safe to do this work. Please take the reins and guide us so that Your purposes are accomplished" recognizes the sovereignty of God and brings you into His wisdom and under His protection.

Once you have prayed, you are ready to enter the spiritual realm, but first I want to mention a few more things, then I will get down to the nitty gritty.

Not the Nitty Gritty, But Important

There is a relatively new protocol for intercessory prayer called courts of heaven. This approach to intercession was not being practiced when I first began conducting generational restorations. I know of only one man, the late Dr. Tom Hawkins of *Restoration In Christ Ministries*, who was accessing the high court of heaven in order to present heavenly appeals at the time that I began to learn about this topic. As far as I know, and I may be wrong, he was the first to develop a courtroom strategy, and he did it on behalf of people who were recovering from ritual abuse. He told me that they needed a very safe approach to the Lord in order to receive deliverance and healing. He was kind enough to take the time to teach me how to access the high court of heaven for heavenly appeals.

It was years later that I added the ever-developing courts of heaven intercessory prayer strategy to my toolbox. But to be completely honest, I have only ever needed the throne room of grace, the high court, and the Cross to conduct a solid generational restoration. In later chapters, I will discuss a few other courts of heaven strategies that are worth including in a restoration, but I will mainly stick with the simplest approach possible by keeping to the throne room of grace, the high court, and the Cross. This is because generational restorations can be confusing. There is no point in adding to that confusion by adding complicated methods when simpler methods will do the job. Always keep in mind that God Himself is working to cleanse and restore. Sometimes we make the mistake of leaning on a method and not on His person.

Before we start, let me explain the difference between a heavenly appeal and a generational restoration.

A Heavenly Appeal

A heavenly appeal is a carefully constructed intercessory prayer using legal language such as that found in the Old Testament (see Psalm 82). It is usually written and meant to be read aloud with pauses to listen for direction from the Holy Spirit. The appeal includes many references to scripture as support for why the court should grant the specific requests within the appeal. I have written and offered heavenly appeals on the behalf of others with varying results. In most cases, the request was granted and the person seeking the court's favor received it. But in other cases, the appeal went unanswered. For me, a heavenly appeal is the last thing I try when nothing else has helped.

Now, there is no reason to wait until nothing else has worked to make an appeal. To be honest, the main reason I wait to offer them is because I do not enjoy writing them. Do not be like me! Whenever the Holy Spirit suggests that an appeal would be helpful is the time to craft one. I have included an example of a heavenly appeal as an appendix in the back of the book. Feel free to build off of it.

A Generational Restoration

A restoration also seeks the favor of the court but the purpose is different. A restoration is not for the immediate benefit of a person or persons. It seeks to remove the lies and filth that sin has deposited upon an entire bloodline so that the glory that God has invested in the tribe may be released. As you can imagine, restorations take longer than presenting an appeal. Deliverance and healing do result from an effective generational restoration, but the purpose is much broader than seeking relief from a single difficult problem.

Now For the Nitty Gritty

You have prayed and now you are ready to come boldly into the throne room of grace.

> *Therefore let us draw near with confidence to the throne of grace, so that we may receive mercy and find grace to help in time of need.*
>
> Hebrews 4:16 ESV

Hebrews 4:16 is an open invitation to enter God's throne room. The throne room is described as a place where we may receive mercy. Mercy is important because you are about to dig into a tribal belief system that will inevitably be hostile toward God. Grace — 'charis' in Greek — means "that which affords joy, pleasure, delight, sweetness, charm, loveliness: grace of speech, and good will."[9] So this throne room is filled with God's mercy and His grace. In other words, He is really glad to see you. Your presence makes Him happy. The directive to enter with confidence also means to enter without fear of speaking honestly. This is a very good place to start your restoration.

---

9   James Strong, *Strong's Expanded Exhaustive Concordance of the Bible*, (Nashville: Thomas Nelson, 2009), G5485.

From time to time, as the restoration progresses, I direct whoever I am praying with back to the throne room of grace to get more clarity, ask questions, or even to just get a hug. It is also a courtroom where petitions may be made and direction received. It is the place I always start every restoration.

So, let us go into the throne room of grace and see what the Lord has to show us. Once we have entered the throne room, we are in God's hands. This is when we will begin to experience spiritual realities.

Common Experiences Within the Throne Room of Grace

Different people experience this place within the spiritual realm differently. And what they experience may change on subsequent visits. As a rule, people are aware that Father God is enthroned here. They may be aware of other spiritual beings such as angels. But what is more important for our purposes is paying attention to the oddities that you see, hear, and feel in the throne room. It is not uncommon for visits to the throne room to be unpleasant. Strong emotions such as shame, fear, and resentment may surface. Feeling that God is angry or indifferent is common. Confusing images may occur. Why do you think that happens?

Please remember Chapters 2 and 3. God speaks to us through symbols, metaphors, and similes. If you see an angry God when you enter the throne room of grace, what might that be a picture of? What might the tribal heart believe about God? As soon as you purpose to cleanse your generational line, God will begin to show you what the heart of your tribe believes. So do not be surprised and do not draw back if the impressions you experience are not loving or kind.

Every feeling, vision, impression, and sound that you experience while in the throne room of grace needs to be carefully examined. The scripture is clear that God has issued you an invitation to join Him there. He has also promised that you will be received with mercy and find grace there — that is, His joyful acceptance. When disturbing emotions and confusing images are experienced, look at them two ways. First, treat what you are experiencing as a manifestation of the tribal heart belief system. *This is what your people believe.* Second, our hearts store inner vows that lock belief systems into place. So, ask the Lord if you are seeing and feeling heart beliefs that will hinder the generational cleanse. For example, *no one helps me (us)* is a heart belief that should be cleaned up before you embark on a restoration.

Since you have entered the throne room of grace for the purpose of starting a generational restoration, now is not the time for a deep dive into your personal traumatic memories. I recommend working on those at another time. If personal memories do surface and are persistent, I would ask the Lord how they apply to the generational restoration.

Keep your focus on receiving useful information, treating the images and feelings you experience in the throne room as helpful clues pointing to the tribal heart belief system.

Clearing Blockages That Surface in the Throne Room of Grace[10]

The first step in clearing a path to the Father on His throne is repentance for the lies that have been believed about Him. I am a get-to-the-point kind of person so I do not use lots of words when repenting. Whenever I see a negative image of God, I simply repent for believing lies about Him. For example, let's say that I see an image of God that is angry and cruel.

I would repent like this:

> *Father God, please forgive me and my people for believing that You are an angry, cruel God who hurt us and wants to hurt us.*

---

10   At this point may I suggest that you read or reread *The Quiet Heart* and *The Performing Heart*, concentrating your efforts on the inner vow sections.

Then I would break the inner vows that lock such a belief in place. For a more thorough exploration of inner vows and how to remove them, see *The Quiet Heart* and *The Performing Heart*. The YouTube series *Your Identity and the Heart* also explains how to recognize and remove inner vows. Here is a quick overview.

Inner Vows

Inner vows are promises made and stored within the heart. They lock into place what the heart believes, and they also compel some kind of action in an effort to manage the pain of what is believed. Let's use the belief that *no one helps us* as an example. When you approach God for help with a generational restoration, if such a belief is in place, you will have trouble receiving or even recognizing God's help. Your heart will blind you to it.

The vow that locks this belief in place sounds something like this: *We can never forget that no one helps us [because there is something wrong with us.]*[11]

More vows are made in the hopes of managing the pain of what the heart believes. They sound like this: *We will do whatever it takes to not be the people no one helps. We will change and become a different people.* When this does not work, and it never works, the people will vow to give up.

1. The heart belief comes first.
   No one helps us because there is something wrong with us.

2. The vow to never forget follows:
   We can never forget that this is who we are.

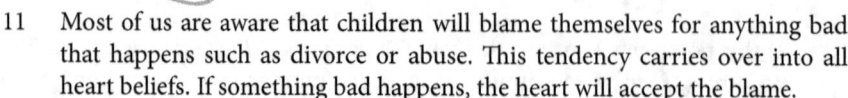

---

[11] Most of us are aware that children will blame themselves for anything bad that happens such as divorce or abuse. This tendency carries over into all heart beliefs. If something bad happens, the heart will accept the blame.

3. The vow to manage the pain follows:
   We will do whatever it takes to stop the hurting.
4. The vow to give up follows:
   We might as well give up because nothing we do changes anything.

Now the tribe is truly trapped in a painful heart belief.

Steps to remove inner vows

I use the following steps to break vows. I suggest speaking each step aloud if possible, although there are times when breaking vows under my breath is necessary and that also works.

1. I break the inner vow to *never forget* that no one helps us because there is something wrong with us.
2. I break the inner vow to *do whatever it takes* to stop the hurting.
3. I break the inner vow to *give up*.
4. I ask the Lord Jesus to empower all the breaking that I have just done.
5. I dismiss all evil spirits attached to the inner vows and I ask the Lord Jesus to break their assignments. I ask You, Jesus, to rebuke them and for You to direct Your holy angels to escort them to Your feet.

Evil spirits attach to inner vows and either amplify the confusion and pain or distract you whenever you seek to discover what the heart believes. So those beings must be removed to a place of submission at the feet of Jesus once the vows are broken.

The most important understanding I want you to take away from this section about the throne room of grace is that God will show you what the tribal heart believes through pictures, sounds, and feelings and that He will use symbols, metaphors, and similes. This is very likely to be uncomfortable and confusing and you will be tempted to draw back.

It will take a bit of determination to recognize what is going on and to take note of all of these spiritual experiences. Keep in mind that the confusing images and emotions experienced in the throne room are helpful clues pointing to the tribal belief system. One more thing. If you become overwhelmed, ask the Lord what you and your people believe about being overwhelmed. Then use the four steps above to break the vows locking what you believe into place. See how that affects your experience in the throne room of grace.

> *It is He who reveals the profound and hidden things. He knows what is in the darkness, and the light dwells with Him.*
>
> Daniel 2:22

Prayer:

> *Lord God, Creator of heaven and earth, I ask You to guide my experiences whenever I enter the throne room of grace. Help me recognize spiritual realities and interpret them for me. Teach me to understand symbols and keep me from automatically leaping to a literal explanation. I am in Your hands and I lean on You as I begin the process of restoring my generational line.*

Practice

1. Ask the Lord to speak to you using symbols from a fantasy realm, such as one you invented, or by books or some other entertainment. Be sure to ask for an interpretation if you do not immediately understand what He is saying through symbolic language.

2. Imagine entering the throne room of grace for the first time. What emotions or images do you anticipate experiencing? How might these reflect your personal or tribal beliefs about God's nature? Do you anticipate Him being loving, distant, or judgmental?

3. Ask the Lord to reveal a heart belief to you. Then ask Him to reveal the inner vows that are locking it into place. Apply the four steps to removing inner vows that are surrounding your heart belief.

CHAPTER 8

ALL RISE; COURT IS IN SESSION

There is only one Lawgiver and Judge …

James 4:12

Now that you have gathered some information about what the tribal heart believes, it is time to ask God for permission to leave the throne room of grace and go into the high court. Simply ask the Lord if He releases you to enter the high court of heaven. Once you have that permission — it may feel like nothing more than a sense that it is ok — step out of the throne room of grace and step into the high court. If you do not receive permission, remain in the throne room and ask why permission has been withheld. Work through any barriers that God brings to mind. After clearing away obstructions and gaining permission, step into the high court. I suggest that you avoid overthinking it. Just say *I am now stepping into the high court of heaven on behalf of* whoever you are working with, if not yourself, in order to cleanse and restore the bloodline.

Remember that I learned my way around the high court before the current courts of heaven intercession strategy had become popular. How I experienced the high court at the beginning was loosely based on a western judicial system. Whenever I go to the high court now, it still appears to me like a traditional American courtroom with a judge seated behind a bench, a witness stand, something that looks like a jury box, and tables facing the bench where attorneys sit or stand. If you are from a different culture, expect this courtroom to resemble that of your culture. This western-style setup has been typical for most courtrooms within the heavenly realm although the furniture and settings vary depending on the purpose of the court and why it has been called into session. If you dive into the courts-of-heaven teaching, you will find many kinds of courtrooms described. But let's leave that aside for now and focus on the high court when it is in session for a generational restoration.

The High Court

God Himself sits as judge over the high court. Because you are His child, you have great favor with Him.

Your purpose is three-fold. You are asking the court for mercy on behalf of your bloodline and for restoration to its original design. You are also bringing an accusation against the demonic for attacking your bloodline with the intention of either twisting or eradicating the expression of God that He has placed there. This means that you are asking for justice.

Evil spirits involved in this crime are on trial. Not you or your tribe. These evil beings have lodged a claim against you and your people because of past sins. They are claiming that sin gives them a legal right to bind all generations to the iniquities, sins, and wrong beliefs committed and established in the past.

It is common for a tribe to agree with the enemy that it deserves to be punished. Such an agreement empowers demonic predation because it gives permission to the enemy. The Cross of Jesus is the answer whenever you discover that your tribe is accepting punishment from the demonic. I will explain more on that later. As you conduct your cleanse, look for beliefs and agreements that open doors to the demonic.

Jesus and the Holy Spirit are your legal team. Jesus advocates for your innocence because you have accepted Him as your Savior. The Holy Spirit knows all things and functions as a research attorney who brings all past actions and hidden beliefs to light.

> *But when He, the Spirit of truth, comes, He will guide you into all the truth; for He will not speak on His own, but whatever He hears, He will speak; and He will disclose to you what is to come.*
>
> John 16:13

Unlike some courtrooms in the heavenly realm, the high court is usually quiet and the courtroom is only filled by the people and beings I mentioned above. The evil beings involved are not in the courtroom at the beginning of this proceeding. Let's get settled and then we will have them brought in.

The High Court's Opening Proceedings

1. Enter the high court with your legal team: Jesus and the Holy Spirit.
2. Approach the bench where Father God is seated as Judge.
3. Tell the Judge why you are in His court. Like this: *Your Honor, I am here on behalf of my people, seeking to restore the glory You placed upon my bloodline.*
4. Prove that you have standing in this case by stating that you are the natural descendent of the tribe you want to represent. If you have rejected your natural father/mother or family, now is the time to repent for that. You cannot represent your tribe if you have rejected it. Accept openly in the courtroom that the tribe you want restored is your tribe. Agree with God that you share the bloodline so that

He will recognize your right to represent the tribe. I understand why you may have rejected your family. I rejected my father's bloodline because he was abusive, but the Lord showed me that unless I accept that my father is my father, I cannot share in the gifts and glory He had given to my tribe. So, I reluctantly accepted that my father is my natural father. I have not regretted doing that.

5. At this point in the proceedings, explain to the court that you are God's child purchased with the blood of Jesus Christ. If you are working with someone else, they can give evidence that you are a follower of Christ. This is necessary because all of us have either committed the sins of our ancestors, been unknowingly complicit in those sins, and agreed with the belief system handed down to us. Establishing that you are the blood-bought child of God gives you special protection, status, and standing in the court. Jesus Himself is backing you up.

6. Ask the Judge if He will hear your case. When He agrees (and He always does) it is time for your accusers to be brought into the courtroom.

The Accusers become the Accused

I mentioned that I sense the presence of something like a jury box within the high courtroom. This box functions as a holding area for the evil spirits that targeted your tribe so many years ago. There is no need for a jury during a generational restoration. But there is a need for a holding area. Ask the court to have every evil spirit, from highest to the lowest, involved in injuring your tribe to be brought into the courtroom and seated in the holding area. Ask the Lord to rebuke any that step out of line. You will sense these beings as they are escorted into the courtroom. Do not engage with them. These beings, because they worked against God to circumvent His will for your people, are to be held accountable for their actions. Leave them for now. We will return to them at the end of the cleanse and restoration.

The Cleansing, the Healing, and the Restoration

Begin the work of restoration by asking the court to give you a container filled with the exact cleansing, healing, and restoration your tribe needs. As an aside, I work with one side of the family at a time. While in the throne room of grace, ask the Lord which side He wants to start with — father or mother. It is a good idea to cleanse both sides but at different times. Generationals are challenging enough so anything that lessens the confusion is good. Working on one side at a time is best.

Pay close attention to what you are given when you ask for the container of blessings. This is another moment when spiritual realities specific to your bloodline will manifest. Hints and clues about what your tribe believes will appear at this time as well as clues about the generational gifting on the bloodline. Anything can happen. I have conducted generationals when nothing was given to the person asking. In other generationals the container given was filled with disturbing or seemingly useless objects. And sometimes the person is handed things of great beauty or import. In all of these cases, it was a moment to stop and ask for clarification about what these things represent.

When nothing is given ask: *What are You showing me? What does my tribe believe that must be resolved before we go any further?*

In such instances, it is common for the tribe to believe that God is not willing to help or has abandoned it. It also possible the tribe believes that they do not deserve anything good.

When the objects appear to be useless ask again: *What are You showing me? What does my tribe believe?* It is possible the tribe believes that any help they are given is worthless. You will ask these kinds of questions during the entire cleanse.

Keep in mind that God speaks most often through symbolism, metaphor, and simile, all of which require interpretation. Take your time as you are given clues to the tribal belief system. It is important to avoid leaping to conclusions. You are seeking to discover what your tribe believes about itself, about relationships, and about life. Because of the fall, tribal heart belief systems (and personal heart belief systems) are built in a desperate effort to manage overwhelming confusion and avoid pain. These systems go deep and are hidden from our conscious mind. Much becomes clear as you continue with the restoration.

> *For He (God) knows the secrets of the heart.*
>
> Psalm 44:21

> *I, the Lord, search the heart …*
>
> Jeremiah 17:10

Then there are cases when nothing happens and everything feels and seems blank. There is a good possibility the tribal heart belief will include the view that they are nothings or that there is nothing good for them or that God thinks of them as nothings. But sometimes it is caused by blocking vows. Here is what to do when this happens.

When Everything Is Blank

There are certain kinds of vows that block access to what the heart believes. These blocking vows serve to manage overwhelming confusion and pain by deciding to just never acknowledge what the tribe believes. It induces a kind of intentional amnesia.

Here is a list of the vows that block access to heart belief systems. I am going to use the plural since this book is about the tribal heart. More on blocking vows may be found in my previous books.

Blocking Vows

In order to access the tribe's belief system blocking vows need to be removed. Blocking vows sound like this.

> *We will do whatever it takes to not remember, not go there, not know it, not hear it, not see it, not feel it, not think it, not speak it, not want it, and not do it. We will do whatever it takes to not be this people. We will become someone else. We will keep what happened and what we believe hidden and secret.*

As you can see, these kinds of promises, once agreed to by the tribe, unravels reality, denies the truth, and creates almost impenetrable walls between you and what your tribe believes. My practice is to break all blocking vows whenever I hit any amplified confusion and distractions, roadblocks, or the dreaded nothing. Here is how to break blocking vows.

> *I break all vows we made as a people to do whatever it takes to not remember, not go there, not know it, not hear it, not see it, not feel it, not think it, not speak it, not want it, and not do it. I break all vows we made to do whatever it takes to not be this people; to remake ourselves into something better. I break the vows we made to keep what happened and what we believe hidden and secret.*
>
> *I ask Jesus to empower the words I have just spoken and activate the breaking.*

Now include this important part.

> *I break the assignment of all evil spirits attached to these vows and I reassign them to the feet of Jesus. Angels, take them there now. Again I ask Jesus to empower the words I have just spoken and activate the breaking.*

Once the blocking vows are removed, ask again for your container of blessings. If you still do not receive it, ask the Judge what the tribe believes about being a nothing and/or having nothing. Explore that set of beliefs until you are able to receive the blessings that God wants you to distribute to your bloodline. If you are still unable to receive from the court, proceed with the generational by asking for the blood of Jesus to be your blessing. As a matter of fact, all of us can add that to our container of cleansing, healing, and restoration.

Once you have received your container of blessings and feel reasonably confident that you understand what it contains — more clarity will come as you go along — it is time to step into the past.

> But the Advocate, the Holy Spirit, whom the Father will send in My name, will teach you all things and will remind you of everything I have said to you.
>
> John 14:26 NIV

Let's pray:

> Lord God, the only Judge and Lawgiver, I ask You to guide me as I approach You on behalf of my tribe. Please open my senses to spiritual realities and open my mind to the interpretations You give me. Take the pain and confusion that would stop me from this work. Give me persistence and courage. Help me know that Jesus and the Holy Spirit are right here with me. Amen.

Practice

1. Visit the throne room of grace and ask the Lord for permission to enter the high court. Practice stepping into the throne room of grace, stepping out, and stepping into the high court. Just practice. Do not start a generational yet.
2. Rehearse breaking the blocking vows and reassigning evil spirits to Jesus' feet.
3. Make a list of blocking vows and keep it with you whenever you are conducting a generational.
4. Stand in the high court and pray for mercy on your bloodline, calling on the blood of Jesus and His finished work to advocate for you.

CHAPTER 9

THE FRAMEWORK

... God is greater than our heart, and He knows all things.

1 John 3:20

THIS CHAPTER IS DEVOTED TO EXPLAINING the structure upon which I build a generational. What you experience, see, hear, and feel — the spiritual realities you encounter as you conduct your generational will vary widely. Because of this I cannot predict what you will experience. Therefore, my emphasis is on providing you with a solid and tested structure that includes steps to help you navigate the mysteries of a generational restoration. This structure simply provides a framework designed to limit confusion while helping you stay focused on your goal of discovering what is within the tribal heart. What you discover is much more important than the structure. But without some sort of structure, along with a step-by-step process, a generational restoration devolves into chaos.

Here is where you are so far.

> You have your healing, cleansing, and restoration blessings.
>
> You have your legal team with you — Jesus and the Holy Spirit.
>
> You have your starting point — the Tower of Babel.
>
> You have your goal — You are seeking to discover the hidden beliefs buried within the tribal heart. You are going to address those beliefs in order to cleanse your bloodline and release the glory God has embedded within its spiritual DNA.

You are looking specifically for beliefs falling into three categories.

1. What the tribe believes about itself — identity
2. What the tribe believes about others — relationships, including how the tribe perceives God.
3. What the tribe believes about life — what will always happen to us.

Let's get started by asking the Holy Spirit to take you back in time to the Tower of Babel. That is the starting point of this structured method. Once you sense that you are at that place in time, ask Him to place you within the timeline that belongs to either your father's or mother's tribe. You are going to follow that timeline to the present day.

Keep it simple. Just ask like this:

> *Holy Spirit, please take me back in time to the Tower of Babel and place me at the beginning of my tribe's timeline.*

Once you sense that you are standing at the beginning of your timeline, you are going to go forward by releasing the blessings that you have been given. I suggest sending them 500 years forward in time. Like this:

> *I release cleansing, healing, and restoration to my bloodline. I send it down 500 years. I ask Jesus of Nazareth, the Redeemer of my tribe, to activate the words I have just spoken.*

Spiritual Realities and the Tribal Heart

This first pass down your timeline is meant to discover where you actually need to begin the generational. Not every bloodline gets into serious trouble right out of the Tower of Babel gate. But problems usually do show up within the first 500 years of the tribe's existence, often much sooner.

Watch what happens as the blessing rolls down the timeline. You are looking for spiritual realities to manifest. Take note of what you discern as the blessing moves forward. Try to remain focused on learning what the tribe believes. Once you locate the first significant trauma — almost always happens within the first 500 years — start asking questions about what your tribe believed in response to the trauma. Stop and work there to resolve those beliefs, then send the blessing down the next 500 years and so on. The Tower of Babel happened around 2250 BC so you have about 4275 years to cleanse and restore. Plan on cleansing both sides of your generational line.

As you cleanse, I promise that you will not only find the bad stuff. Sometimes there are stored blessings waiting to be released. And the unique gifting given to your tribe should become increasingly apparent as you resolve the painful beliefs held within the tribal heart. This gifting is how your tribe is designed to express the goodness of God in the earth. But first, let's get cleaned up.

I will explain more on how to recognize and resolve tribal heart beliefs in the next chapter. Putting a process and structure in place first is very important.

Here is the process in steps.

1. Ask the Holy Spirit to take you back in history to the Tower of Babel.
2. Once there, ask Him to place you at the beginning of your tribal timeline.
3. Once you sense that you are standing at the beginning of your timeline, release the blessing you were given in the high court,

sending it forward 500 years. You are looking for the first significant trauma.

4. See what spiritual realities manifest and take note, remaining focused on discovering what your tribe believed about itself, others, and life as a result of the trauma.

5. Continue the process, until you arrive at the present day.

6. Extend the restoration to all living descendants of the tribe and send it forward 1000 generations to those yet born.

Here is the structure.

1. Start at the Tower of Babel. This is your starting point.

2. Take your stance at the beginning of your tribe's timeline.

3. Release the blessing from the beginning (where you are standing) forward 500 years in order to locate the genesis of the beliefs held within the tribal heart.

4. Once located, move to that place in the timeline and focus your attention on the heart beliefs of the tribe as they developed. Work there until you feel a release.

5. Send the restoration blessing down the next 500 years.

6. Continue until you arrive at the present day.

What to look for

As humanity organized itself into tribes and traveled away from the Tower of Babel and into an unexplored earth, they carried within themselves a traumatic memory of a devastating flood. From their behavior at the Tower, it is to be supposed that they blamed God for that flood and not their own sinfulness. In all likelihood, they also blamed God for suddenly confusing their language and dividing them into tribes. No doubt it was a very traumatic experience. My point is that your tribe was already predisposed to hold fear and resentment toward God. As they suffer other traumas, that fear and resentment will mature into hard-held heart beliefs against God. Keep your eye out for those beliefs.

The first thing to watch for as you roll your blessing down the first 500 years are bumps, roadblocks, ditches, and pits. Bumps will affect the movement of the blessing, roadblocks will stop it, and your blessing will fall into the ditches and pits. Each of these impediments are a signal to you to stop and ask questions. The first question to ask the Holy Spirit is *what happened to my people?* If you just cannot get an answer that makes sense, break the blocking vows that are listed in Chapter 8 and ask again.

Knowing what happened to your people is secondary to knowing what they *believed* as a result of what happened. But it does make it easier to figure out the belief system when you know the events that led up to the tribe's actions and decisions. But it is not essential to know anything in detail. A broad understanding of the event or circumstances is enough.

In some cases, what happened to the tribe is clear from the beginning. In others, the trauma is hidden behind blocking vows. Some people see what happened as if they are watching a drama unfold. Others get flashes of images and impressions and/or get a feeling about what happened. Any way you receive information is fine. When you begin to get a sense of the event or circumstances that launched painful heart beliefs, ask the Lord questions like this:

> *What did my people believe when the bad thing happened? What did they believe about themselves? How did this shape their identity?*

Then move to questions about relationships.

> *What did my people decide about how others will behave? What do they expect to happen in their relationships? How will others treat them? What did they believe about You because of the trauma?*

Next, ask questions about life.

> *What do my people believe about how life will treat them? What do they expect will always happen to them?*

Once you have the basic outline of the heart belief system, you can begin to understand that the sin patterns inherent on the generational line are the result of the tribe's belief system. Another way of saying that is the fruit (sin) that you see being produced generation after generation is growing from the root which is the belief system. Resolve the belief system and the sin will die.

As you travel down your timeline, you will discover that the original trauma, around which the tribe's belief system formed, will repeat in other similar traumas. This is because the tribe believes within its corporate heart that life will always go badly for them in that certain way. They will continue to *always* be treated by others in the way that they expect and they will continue to see themselves as victims of that first trauma. My point is this. The tribal heart belief system forms as the tribe responds to significant trauma. That trauma can be anything — famine, drought, plague, attacks, and any meaningful loss such as loss of land, resources, honor, or even the loss of a leader. Any trauma that causes the tribe to believe that *they cannot recover* will result in the development of a painful heart belief system that will be handed down to subsequent generations.

Here is a list of common traumas

Famine and drought

Plague and disease

Natural disaster

Loss of land (being driven or taken from land)

Loss of position and the honor that came with it

Attacks that lead to death, slavery, loss of resources, dishonor

Sudden loss of a beloved leader, the heir apparent, tribe members

Abandonment by the tribe's men or women

Profound dishonor of the men or women

And there are probably other traumas that happened as the tribes went away from the Tower of Babel.

Now that you have a basic structure in place for your generational, and before I get into the spiritual realities you are most likely to experience as well as how to recognize heart beliefs and what to do with those heart beliefs, I want to explain something important. The best way that I know how to explain it is to make a comparison. This comparison is a metaphor.

Have you ever needed physical therapy? If you have you will understand this comparison. After your first session, the therapist hands you several sheets of paper with pictures and directions for exercises to be done at home. Sounds easy enough until you get home and try to figure out how to do the exercises on the papers. Doing them under the guidance of a knowledgeable therapist is one thing. Trying to translate the written instructions into actual exercises is a completely different animal. My husband has been through a lot of physical therapy, and I have had some as well. Both of us complain about how difficult it is to interpret the instructions and pictures. We do our best, wondering if we are doing the exercises correctly, then at our next appointments go back to the therapist with our sheets of paper, asking for further explanations.

Giving you these instructions on how to conduct a generational restoration feels to me a lot like handing you an instruction sheet, patting you on the shoulder while saying, "You can do it, tiger."

Like physical therapy, generational restorations are a physical, hands on, all emotions and senses involved activity. There is no way that any written explanation can transfer what it feels like to be immersed in the spiritual realm and be experiencing sometimes strange and puzzling spiritual realities as the history of your bloodline is unveiled before your eyes. The best I can do is offer you a basic structure and some steps that work for me. To truly understand the immensity and significance of a generational restoration, you will have to plunge into the spiritual realm and just do your best. The Holy Spirit is your therapist. He will explain and guide and help you. Whenever you are confused — and confusion comes with the territory — break the blocking vows and ask Him to explain.

> *Trust in the Lord with all your heart*
> *And do not lean on your own understanding.*
> *In all your ways acknowledge Him,*
> *And He will make your paths straight.*
>
> Proverbs 3:5–6

Let's pray.

> *Father God, Creator of all, I am so grateful that You have placed me within a bloodline that is uniquely designed. Because of the fall, tragedies and many wrong beliefs have overtaken us. Thank You for teaching me to cleanse my tribe so that these trauma-based beliefs rule no longer. Help me cleanse and restore my tribal heart. With thankfulness, I pray in Jesus' name.*

Practice

1. Write out the process and structure of the generational restoration that you have learned so far.

2. Ask your heart what beliefs about God you have hidden away. Ask the Lord to help you examine those beliefs honestly.

3. Ask your heart to bring to mind a childhood trauma. Ask your heart what you really believe about that trauma. Do you believe that you can recover from it? Ask the Lord to speak to your heart about recovering from trauma. How does the childhood trauma and the beliefs that resulted from it repeat the patterns of tribal heart beliefs and trauma?

CHAPTER 10

THE TIMELINE

For the Lord searches all hearts ...

1 Chronicles 28:9

THE SCOPE AND VARIETY OF spiritual realities that you may encounter as you conduct a generational restoration is without measure. Because of this, I will limit myself to explaining the most common spiritual realities you are likely to experience as you travel down your tribe's timeline. Keep to the structure I explained in Chapter 9. This structure will keep you from becoming lost in too many possibilities and will help you conduct a more thorough cleanse. Stay focused on discovering what the tribal heart believes. What the tribe believes is more important than what happened to the tribe. As you conduct your restoration, you will discern many spiritual realities. It is easy to fall in love with spiritual experiences. Pray to avoid that. Keep in mind that spiritual realities are meant to be interpreted. Lean on the Holy Spirit. I think that you will find that the simplest explanation is usually the correct one.

Bumps, Roadblocks, Ditches, and Pits

As you roll your generational blessing down the timeline you will probably discern that timeline as a path or road. Pay attention to any barriers that stop the blessing from continuing along that path. These barriers are most often experienced as bumps — in which case the blessing continues but skews off to the side or moves in an uncertain fashion — or roadblocks which stop the blessing completely. These are often seen as mountains, boulders, or other impassable obstacles. You may discern ditches alongside the timeline that the blessing veers into or pits that it falls into. Each of these barriers indicates that something significant occurred at that moment in time.

You are at the beginning of your generational restoration, so it is highly likely that the first barrier you encounter marks the first trauma or that critical point when the tribe responded to trauma in the wrong way. Step down the timeline to the place where the restoration blessing was interrupted. Look closely at the barrier. Look with your eyes and listen with your ears. Pay close attention to your emotions because you may experience the emotions that your ancestors felt at that time. Do not be surprised if you feel confusion, fear, helplessness, resentment, despair, rage, and so on. Try to avoid applying these emotions to something happening in real time. Instead ask the Lord to show you why you are feeling what you are feeling. What are these emotions meant to reveal?

With your senses engaged, ask the Lord to show you what happened. Usually, a scene will unfold or the Holy Spirit will give you a download of information that reveals the trauma and the resulting decisions affecting the tribe. Be especially aware of decisions that have the potential of developing into a shared heart belief system. Pain is always the result of a trauma-based belief system.

A pain-filled heart belief system will direct the tribe toward behaviors designed to contain and manage the pain of what is believed. These behaviors become the patterns of sin that repeat from generation to generation. Here is another way of saying it: What the tribe believes within its heart acts like a root from which grows a tree that produces fruit. The fruit is patterns of sin afflicting the tribe generation after generation. When the root is exposed and destroyed, the tree dies, and no more fruit is produced.

It is the wrong beliefs that lead to sinful actions. Those actions may include striking bargains with demonic forces. I will cover how to dismantle such agreements, but keep in mind always that it was the wrong beliefs that led to the agreements. Removing the agreements without confronting and changing the wrong beliefs is like casting out a demon and leaving the house empty — all swept and made clean so that the demon can return with a half dozen friends and take up residence once more.

As you examine the barrier, you may not discern anything. If that happens, ask the Lord to break the blocking vows and then ask again. If you continue to see, hear, and feel nothing I suggest that you explore the possibility that your tribe believes it is a nothing that has nothing and can expect nothing. Such heart beliefs are sometimes discerned by experiencing an extreme and impenetrable sense of nothing. Once again, ask the Lord to break the vows holding these beliefs in place, then ask Him why did the people of my tribe believe they were a nothing? (Please review how to break inner vows in Chapter 7). This question should take you to the traumas and decisions that resulted in the belief.

As the Lord reveals your tribal history, begin asking Him to tell you what your people believed in the midst of the trauma. Your focus is on discovering and dismantling the heart belief system. You are going to experience many spiritual realities. Do not let wondrous spiritual experiences cause you to lose your focus.

Bumps, roadblocks, ditches, and pits are useful for pinpointing when the tribe made decisions that affected or reinforced the belief system. As you move your restoration beyond the first 500 years, it is highly probable that you will continue to encounter these kinds of barriers. Always stop and explore. Ask the Holy Spirit to explain why the blessing has stopped or been altered. Remember to ask, "What did my tribe believe?"

The Path and the Landscape

The next thing to look at is the path itself and the landscape along the sides of the path. It is very common for people to see a smooth path and a lush landscape at the very beginning of their generational restoration. This vision changes to reflect developing heart beliefs. Usually it changes to a narrow, rocky path and a barren landscape. Sometimes there is no path at all. Just emptiness. Keep in mind that most of what we discern is symbolic. Also keep in mind that what a symbol means to you may not mean the same thing to someone else. Nevertheless, a difficult path and a barren landscape are symbols that always represent what a tribe believes. It is essential for you to ask the Lord why the path appears as it does and why the landscape appears barren, devastated, or empty. Something bad has happened. It is very likely that the tribe believes they are ruined and cannot recover from something bad.

Bumps, roadblocks, ditches, and pits help to locate the place in the timeline where the original trauma occurred. They also flag later significant events and decisions that affected the belief system or reinforce the existing belief system. Paths and landscapes do not identify trauma; they represent what the tribe believes about life.

Once you have gained an understanding of the original trauma, it is time to focus your attention on the tribal heart beliefs.

[God] knows all things.

1 John 3:20

The Heart is a Control Center

Why am I so loudly beating a drum about the importance of heart beliefs? Let's look at scripture, then I will explain.

The physical human heart ('lēḇ' in Hebrew, 'kardia' in Greek) is mentioned in the Bible over 1000 times. Scripture teaches us that we believe with the heart and that the heart manages what we believe (Romans 10:10; Proverbs 4:23). What we believe within the heart strongly influences, to the point of controlling, how we perceive reality. I want you to look at some different translations of Proverbs 4:23 to make my point clearer.

> *Guard your heart above all else, for it determines the course of your life.* (NLT)
>
> *Keep your heart with all vigilance, for from it flow the springs of life.* (ESV)
>
> *Above all else, guard your heart, for everything you do flows from it.* (NIV)

The heart is to be vigilantly guarded ABOVE ALL ELSE! This strongly suggests that your heart is a major player in the outcomes of your life. Now consider the phrases "determines the course" and "everything you do." Nothing is left out. The heart is a control center affecting every area of your life. Remember Identity, Relationships, and Life? Yes. Those things.

Now consider the words translated as *course, flows,* and *sources.* These words mean the *outgoings* of your heart or the stuff that comes out of your heart. What are those outgoings? What is flowing from your heart? Take a look at Mark 7:18–23. Jesus is talking.

> *Do you not understand that whatever goes into the man from outside cannot defile and dishonor him, since it does not enter his heart, but his stomach, and is eliminated? ...* **Whatever comes**

> ***from the heart of a man***, *that is what defiles and dishonors him. For from within, **out of the heart** of men, come base and malevolent thoughts and schemes, acts of sexual immorality, thefts, murders, adulteries, acts of greed and covetousness, wickedness, deceit, unrestrained conduct, envy and jealousy, slander and profanity, arrogance and self-righteousness and foolishness (poor judgment). All these evil things [schemes and desires] come from within and defile and dishonor the man."* (AMP)

Yikes! The heart is capable of storing some pretty awful things (Matthew 12:35). Here is a question. How did those evil things get inside the heart?

Recall that we believe with the heart. This means that the heart controls our perception of reality because it stores what we believe. Because of the fall, our hearts hold wrong beliefs. The issues of life flow through the wrong beliefs held within the heart, turning the clear water of reality into murky swamp water. We then understand and interact with ourselves, others, and life based upon the wrong beliefs stored within our hearts.

Believing with the heart is not automatically a bad thing. It is a good thing if our beliefs line up with a godly understanding of creation. But belief systems are established when we are very small children, responding to often traumatic and certainly confusing circumstances. This leads us to believe bad things. When we believe bad things, we act out in bad ways. That is how the evil stuff Jesus listed gets inside our hearts and also how evil stuff gets inside the tribal heart.

As individuals we have responded in wrong ways to our personal circumstances. The ancient tribes also responded in wrong ways to the challenges they faced. Their wrong responses eventually solidified into heart belief systems that are inherited by their offspring. This inherited belief system greatly influences the development and flavor of your personal heart belief system. Discovering, confronting, and resolving wrong tribal heart beliefs lifts quite a weight off of your heart and is an important, in my opinion essential, part of your healing journey.

OK! I am done beating on my drum. Let's learn how to recognize all-important heart beliefs.

How To Recognize Tribal Heart Beliefs

Let's go back to the beginning of your generational timeline and roll that restoration blessing down to a place that feels off in some way. Perhaps you hit a roadblock or you discern that this is a place to stop. Stand there (spiritually speaking), asking the Lord what happened. As you gain insight into a trauma of some kind, ask the Lord what your tribe believed as they experienced that trauma. I listed possible traumas in Chapter 9, but the trauma to a tribe does not have to be huge. The tribe only has to respond to pain in such a way that wrong beliefs find a place within the tribal heart. For example, the trauma that birthed a devastating tribal heart belief system on my father's side does not seem to be traumatic at first glance.

Here is what happened. As I sought to restore my paternal bloodline, I realized that they suffered from believing that God had withheld something that they desperately wanted. I am convinced that my father's tribe carries *confidence in the provision of God* within its spiritual DNA. The tribe is gifted by God to be very confident that God will provide in every way. It is designed by God to express this confidence and to reveal God as a faithful provider to others.

When God said *no* to something the tribe wanted, the people were more deeply hurt than another tribe would be. This is because the tribe is designed to connect with God through provision. God's *no* to something the tribe desperately wanted felt like a severing of the relationship. The people went from disbelief that God actually had said *no* to feeling crushed. In an effort to manage pain, the tribe nurtured anger and resentment toward God and vowed to *do whatever it took* to get what it wanted.

Giving up on their relationship with God, the people became their own providers. Soon the enemy was twisting and controlling their desires. They began to believe they wanted terrible and harmful things. They cheated, stole, and preyed on the vulnerable. They abused anyone who stood between them and what they wanted. All effort was bent toward getting the one thing they wanted the most. Desire became their god.

Because God does not withdraw His gifts, the tribe's innate ability to confidently rest in God's provision remains, but it is buried beneath the bitter heart belief that God will withhold the one thing that it wants the most. Because He withholds it, the tribe cannot be content. My paternal tribe is the poster child for James 4:1–3

> *What is the source of quarrels and conflicts among you? Is the source not your pleasures that wage war in your body's parts? You lust and do not have, so you commit murder. And you are envious and cannot obtain, so you fight and quarrel. You do not have because you do not ask. You ask and do not receive,* **because you ask with the wrong motives, so that you may spend what you request on your pleasures.**

God has never shown me what my people wanted so badly. He has only told me that if He had given in to our desires that it would have destroyed us as a people.

So, the trauma that profoundly affected your tribe might seem minor to you when you first discover it. Keep examining it, asking questions, and asking the Lord to connect the dots for you.

The Language and Emotion of Heart Beliefs

The easiest way to recognize heart beliefs is found in language. This is because whatever is stored within our hearts — what we believe absolutely — will be expressed in words. Heart belief language is a language of absolutes because the heart is designed to believe without any doubt. The rest of our being — our minds, souls, and spirits may entertain other possibilities. But not the heart. Once the heart believes, it believes completely. Here are some words that reveal when a heart belief is being expressed.

Always, Every Time, Everyone, Everything, No Matter What, No One, and *Never.*

Statements that include these kinds of words are usually accompanied by feelings of resignation.

The heart also speaks in emotionally painful statements of immovable belief. So, when you hear yourself repetitively saying or thinking, "I'm stupid. I'm ugly. I'm bad. I'm unlovable. I'm disgusting. I'm a failure. I'm a loser. I'm weak. I don't have what it takes. I make bad things happen," you are hearing from your heart belief system.

Here are some examples to help you recognize tribal heart beliefs when you hear them either spoken or in your thoughts.

> *We are always mistreated. We are always misunderstood. We are always left out. We always fail. We always lose.*
>
> *Everyone hurts us. Everyone despises us. Everyone takes advantage of us. Everyone hates us.*
>
> *We can never succeed. We can never get ahead. We can never win.*
>
> *No one helps us. No one likes us. No one respects us. No one cares about us.*

Here are some examples of emphatic statements that feel absolutely true.

We are losers. We are weak. We are helpless. We are fools. We are failures.

All heart beliefs are accompanied by a nagging sense of inevitability. Tribal heart beliefs may come with strong emotion — individual heart beliefs certainly come with a bucketful of strong emotion — or they may feel less personal emotionally while still feeling imprinted upon your being.

Remember from previous chapters the tribal belief that *we are the people who are always treated unfairly?* In all likelihood, the tribe formed that belief from one or two bad experiences. If they had been thinking rationally — that is, with the mind and not the heart — it would know that one or two bad experiences does not mean that the tribe will always be treated unfairly. But the heart is not so sophisticated. It functions from an either/or perspective. Once it believes that the tribe is treated unfairly, the heart believes that it will *always* be treated unfairly by *everyone*. Notice the heart language.

Being treated unfairly feels normal for this tribe. It feels woven into the design. It is just who they are, how they will be treated, and how life will flow for them.

As you stop at the bumps, roadblocks, ditches, and pits; as you examine the paths and landscapes; as God unfolds for you the trauma that birthed your tribe's heart belief system, listen for absolute language and feel for the emotions, especially the emotion of inevitability, because language and emotion reveal what the tribe believes.

For his mouth speaks from that which fills his heart.

Luke 6:45

Prayer:

Father God, Creator of heaven and earth, Maker of the human heart. I recognize that the heart is not a bad thing in itself, but what it stores can be an awful mess. Please teach me to be aware of the beliefs hidden within my heart. Help me dismantle the inherited tribal heart beliefs and my own individual beliefs that are not in agreement with godly reality.

In Jesus' name, I ask for Your guidance in this. Amen.

Practice

1. Ask the Holy Spirit to teach you to recognize the language of the heart. Then, for one week, carry a small notebook or use a phone app. When stressed or upset, note any absolute statements that come to mind. For example: "I always mess up. No one listens." Note the statement, along with any emotion, and the context. Ask the Holy Spirit if the belief surfacing is also a tribal heart belief. Journal insights, asking, "How does this reflect what my tribe believes about its identity, relationships, or life?"

CHAPTER 11

ALLIGATORS AND CAROUSELS: DISMANTLING TRIBAL HEART BELIEFS

Blessed are the pure in heart, for they will see God.

Matthew 5:8

I AM NOT EXACTLY SURE how old I was, early elementary school age, so maybe six or seven when my parents took my brother and me to Florida's Silver Springs for our family vacation. Silver Springs is a place of wonder for a young child — the air boat swamp tour, the glass bottom boats, the alligator wrestler. But these marvelous wonders were outshone by the wonder of them all. Baby alligators for sale in the gift shop. Yes. Sixty years ago, back when life was fun, you could buy a baby alligator.

They were such cute little lizards and my young self wanted one more than anything I had ever wanted in my life. I would keep it in the bathtub. When my parents said no and bought me a little plush alligator instead, I was beyond devastated.

I had experienced this deep level of heartbreak before. My father had been transferred from his Alaskan assignment to an assignment in Alabama. My parents decided to travel to Alabama by car, stopping on the way to visit significant landmarks, one of which was Disneyland in Anaheim, California. I think I was five years old. As we prowled through Disneyland, I spotted what I thought were horses. I later learned that they were pack mules and part of the now-closed Frontierland attraction. I begged my parents to let me ride the "horses." They had not seen the mules and thought I wanted to ride the carousel. I cried inconsolably as I was spun around and around on top of a brightly painted fake horse.

So what do alligators and carousels have to do with dismantling a tribal heart belief? Tribal heart beliefs are inherited. If you recall from the previous chapter, my paternal tribe believed that they could never have the one thing they wanted the most. I wanted a baby alligator and a horseback ride more than anything I had wanted before. When those desires were denied, that inherited heart belief activated and crushed me under the accumulated weight of generations of disappointment. It was not long before I was in complete agreement with the heart belief that I had inherited. I believed with all my heart that I could never have the one thing that I wanted the most. Quiet despair haunted me most of my life. This is the power of tribal heart beliefs and the reason I am writing to you.

Hope deferred makes the heart sick ...

Proverbs 13:12

Learning how to recognize the foundational heart belief that determines the course of your tribe's life is essential. But just knowing the belief is not very helpful if you do not also know what to do with it. Discovering the heart belief is the beginning, but for sustainable healing to occur we must dismantle that belief by removing the vows and any attached evil beings, and instructing the heart to replace the belief with God-filtered reality.

Dismantling the structure of heart beliefs is a step-by-step process which means that it can be taught and learned with practice. The reason I take a methodical approach to dismantling heart beliefs is similar to why I structure generational restorations. When conducting a generational restoration, you are working in the spiritual realm on a historical problem that has been lost in time. Confusion is a big issue and the temptation to give up is an even bigger one. Structure offers a measure of order and a logical process that helps to limit the confusion, making it possible to persevere. The heart realm is also confusing with the added distraction of murky unprocessed tribal emotions that surface as you go along. Applying a step-by-step process helps contain the confusion and emotions. Recognizing and dismantling heart beliefs does take practice and there is an element of confusion that must be endured in order to bring down these inherited heart beliefs. I am confident that the Holy Spirit will guide you and give you the needed perseverance.

How To Dismantle a Tribal Heart Belief

I think the best way to teach the dismantling of heart beliefs is by using examples, so I am going to use my paternal tribe's heart belief. Heart beliefs occupy a structure. Tribal and individual heart beliefs are structured in the same way.

The structure of a heart belief

1. The belief
2. The why questions — heart beliefs are followed by questions such as these: *Why is God letting this bad thing happen? We must have done something wrong. What could that be? What is it about us that causes bad things to happen? What is wrong with us?* Basically, the tribe is seeking to understand why God is ok with allowing it to suffer. The answers they arrive at are inevitably wrong.

3. The completed belief — the completed belief combines the heart belief with the answers to the why questions.

4. Vows that lock the belief into place — these vows make it impossible to forget what the tribe believes. They are vows to *never forget*.

5. Vows that manage the pain of the belief — these vows begin with the blocking vows mentioned in Chapter 8, followed by any number of vows that the tribe thinks might help mitigate pain, including the vow to give up.

6. The involvement of evil spirits.

Let's look at that structure again.

The heart belief structure begins with a heart belief. The wrong answers to questions about why the bad thing happened is then added to the heart belief. This is followed by vows to *never forget* what the tribe believes and vows to *do whatever it takes* to manage the pain. These vows open the door to evil spirits.

For the sake of clarification, I am going to fill in this structure with my tribe's heart belief. It might be helpful to take notes. Not so that you can memorize my tribe's heart belief, but to help you grasp the logic behind the structure.

1. The belief — *We are the people who cannot have the one thing that we want the most.*

2. The wrong answers to the why questions — *We cannot have what we want the most because God withholds it. He withholds it because He wants us to suffer. He wants us to suffer because there is something wrong with us. We must be bad people.*

3. The completed belief — *We are the people who cannot have the one thing that we want the most because we are bad.*

4. The vow locking the belief in place — *We can **never forget** that God withholds what we want the most because we are bad.*

5. The vows that manage the pain — *We will **do whatever it takes** to get what we want the most.* This vow was followed eventually by the vow to *give up* because nothing we do ever gets us the one thing that we want the most.

6. The involvement of spirits — Evil spirits attach to these vows and compel the tribe to *never forget* the heart belief and to *do whatever it takes* to manage the pain.

Now that I have filled in the structure with my paternal tribe's heart belief along with the vows taken that locked it into place, the entire system can be dismantled. But before we go any further, I want to take a closer look at the belief structure, specifically at the why questions and the answers to those questions.

Questions arise whenever trauma happens. And they are always the same questions.

Why did this happen to us?

What did we do to make it happen?

What is it about us that made it happen?

Because we live in a fallen world, trauma appears to strike randomly which causes confusion. The heart wants answers so that it knows exactly what to believe.

For it is with your heart that you believe ...

Romans 10:10

The problem is that the heart, in its effort to stop the confusion, settles for the wrong answers. Instead of blaming the fall for the bad things that happen, the heart blames the victim of the trauma as well as assigning blame to God and to other people. This is the main reason children blame themselves when their parents do not love them or if their parents' divorce or even if a parent dies. The child looks at the frightening, incomprehensible things happening and reasons that God should intervene. If He does not stop the bad thing, the child begins to think that something is wrong with him, that he must be so bad or so inconsequential that God does not care if he suffers. It is not long before the heart accepts that the child made the bad thing happen. This kind of thinking is the direct result of the fall and is promoted by evil spirits. Deciding that God does not intervene because He is either punishing you or is indifferent to your suffering is extremely common if not ubiquitous to the human race.

You might be asking why a child or a tribe automatically thinks the worst about God. I want you to think back to the Flood and the Tower of Babel (see Chapter 6). Because of these two cataclysmic events, the heart of humanity is predisposed to believing that God is dangerous and not to be trusted. On the other hand, because of the fall, the heart of humanity is predisposed to believe the worst about itself.

My paternal tribe believed that it caused God to withhold whatever it was it wanted because the people were bad in some hidden way. This wrong answer to the original belief stops confusion but jumpstarts immense pain. As you explore your tribe's heart beliefs, ask the Lord how did my tribe answer the why questions? They are always the same questions:

Why did this happen to us?

What did we do to make it happen?

What is it wrong with us that makes bad things happen?

Now take a look at the vows that manage pain. The question to ask about these kinds of vows is this:

What did my tribe decide to do to manage the pain of what it believes?

As the tribe attempts to process the trauma it is also scrambling for any way to keep the bad thing from ever happening again. My tribe decided to stop relying on God and do whatever it took to get what it wanted. What did your tribe decide to do to manage its pain?

When you have a pretty good idea of the heart belief in its complete form and have some insight into those earliest vows taken to manage pain, you are in a good position to begin dismantling your tribe's foundational heart belief, the belief that is driving the course of your people's lives.

I suggest that you speak aloud as you break the vows, instruct your heart, and remove spirits. I realize this may not always be possible. So just do your best and God will do the rest. Breaking the vows releases the heart so that it can hear and accept the truth about why bad things happen. Here is the truth. Bad things happen because of the fall. Your heart will actually push God away because it believes that God is against you. Clearing out the lies that your tribe believed makes it possible for your heart to shift the blame to the fall and rest in the goodness of God.

The Dismantling Process

I am still using the heart belief of my paternal tribe as a model.

1. Break the vows

I ask the Lord Jesus to empower the words of breaking I am about to speak so that all unholy vows will be dismantled.

I break the inner vow that we took as a people to never forget that we cannot have the one thing that we want the most because God withholds it. He withholds it because we are bad.

I break the inner vow to *do whatever it takes* to get what we want.

I break the inner vow to *give up*.

2. Instruct the heart

(Instructions need to be repeated until your heart agrees with you. This may take days, weeks, or months. Be persistent).

Heart, you will no longer believe that God withholds what we want because we are bad. Bad things happen because of the fall. That is the only reason and the only thing you need to believe about why bad things happen.

You will stop making me believe that God is punishing us. You will allow the Lord God to prove to me that He is good. You will allow Him to bless me and my tribe with everything that we need to live lives of eternal value. You will stop pushing Him away.

You will stop making me believe that we deserve to be punished because we are bad people.

You will stop compelling me to believe that I can never have the one thing that I want the most. You will stop compelling me to get what I want myself.

You will stop compelling me to give up.

Heart, your job is to root and ground me in God's love and grace. That is what you will do from now on.

3. Remove the spirits

I ask the Lord Jesus to break the assignment of all evil spirits attached to this belief and to cancel these vows on the Cross. I ask Him to direct His holy angels to escort them to His feet.

… Jesus sat down at the right hand of God, and since that time He waits for His enemies to be made His footstool.

Hebrews 10:12–13 NIV

> *Are not all angels ministering spirits sent to serve those who will inherit salvation?*
>
> Hebrews 1:14 NIV

The lies my tribe believed about God and about itself resulted in severing it from its identity. No longer did my tribe release into the earth the love of Father God through provision. Instead, we became predators, resentful toward God, taking from others what God would have gladly given us if we had just been willing to love Him more than we loved our desires.

At no time did God want to be separated from my tribe, but because my tribe *believed* that He wanted to be separate, we lived as if He was. Remember that it is not what happens to a tribe, it is what the tribe believes that determines the outcome.

Let's pray:

> *Lord God, Maker of heaven and earth, You know the secrets of the heart. There is nothing hidden from You. I am beginning to see that the beliefs hidden within my heart determine the course of my life. I am beginning to understand that I am in agreement with the painful lies that my ancestors believed. I ask You to reveal to me what my heart believes and what the heart of my tribe believes. Help me dismantle all heart beliefs that lead to sin and bring dishonor. Amen.*

> *For He knows the secrets of the heart.*
>
> Psalm 44:21

Practice

1. Do you remember this tribal heart belief? *We are the people who will always be treated unfairly.* Take this belief and fit it into the belief structure that is outlined in this chapter. Think about a possible trauma that might have resulted in the belief.

2. Here is another common tribal heart belief that profoundly affects the relationship between men and women. Once you have completed the first practice, try fitting this belief into the structure: *Women are expendable.* What trauma might have resulted in a tribe believing this about women? What do you imagine the consequences would be as a result of this belief?

3. Stand at the beginning of your timeline. Roll your restoration blessing down until you discern a stopping point. Investigate that moment to learn what happened and what your tribe believed about what happened. Write out your tribe's heart belief by using the steps in this chapter. Then dismantle the belief by following the steps under the section ***The Dismantling Process.***

CHAPTER 12

RECONCILIATION

For the inward thought and the heart of a person are deep.

Psalm 64:6

NOW THAT YOU KNOW HOW to recognize a heart belief and how to dismantle it, it is time to continue the restoration process. Once again position yourself at the head of your timeline. Roll your restoration blessing to the moment when your tribe made the decision to believe a life-altering lie. Listen for the absolute language of the heart (see Chapter 10) and work on dismantling the belief structure until you feel that the Lord has released you to move on. Do not be surprised if the Holy Spirit asks you to revisit this first wrong belief and the trauma surrounding it. In all likelihood you will revisit it many times because it functions as the fountainhead for all subsequent decisions and actions.

For example, my father's tribe believed it could never have what it wanted the most, so it vowed to do whatever it takes to get it. As the years went by, the tribe felt compelled to cheat, steal, and manipulate in order to get what it desired. I could spend lots of energy repenting for those sins and seeking healing for the resulting traumas, but if I fail to shut off the fountainhead, I will not gain sustainable freedom. All that to say this. Find the foundational lie. All sin, trauma, and lesser heart beliefs flow from that lie.

I would like to point out that God told my tribe no only once! But the tribe wanted what it wanted so badly that it bargained with God in an effort to change His mind. When God refused to change His mind, the heart became involved. Remember that the heart is already primed to believe that God is against it (see Chapter 6). Also, remember that the heart is an all-or-nothing believer. The heart automatically translates God's *no* into the belief that God *always* says *no* to the one thing the tribe wants the most. This then morphs into the belief that God is *always* against the tribe.

Thus, the tribe believes it can *never* have what it wants the most because God does not want the people to be happy. If I intensely desire a pet baby alligator or a ride on a real horse, my tribal heart is triggered because, in that moment, it is the one thing that I want the most, so of course I cannot have it. Once my heart is locked into this tribal belief, I begin to be compelled to want what I cannot have and compelled to do whatever it takes to get it. Add in the belief that the reason I cannot have what I want is because I am bad, and I am doubly miserable. I think this is the reason Proverbs 4:23 warns us to guard our hearts above all else.

Lesser Heart Beliefs

As you proceed down your timeline, you will encounter other heart beliefs that radiate from that foundational wrong belief. A lesser heart belief that my paternal tribe accepted was that *no one can be trusted.* This belief formed in response to the tribe members' behaviors as they attempted to get what they wanted. As time went by, the enemy twisted the wants of the tribe so that they desired profane things which fits into the heart belief that they are bad.

Keep your senses on alert for lesser heart beliefs that formed in response to sinful actions and other traumas. These lesser heart beliefs are dismantled the same way as that first foundational wrong belief. Just know that the first tribal heart belief is driving the perception of all of life's ups and downs.

It is not unusual to find lesser heart beliefs before you figure out the first foundational wrong belief. This happens when the foundational wrong belief is so painful that the tribe buries it very deeply behind blocking vows (see Chapter 8). In that case, break the blocking vows and send away the attached spirits.

Sometimes removing the blocking vows does not result in clarity. This is usually because we are misinterpreting the symbols or misunderstanding the information God is giving us. When that fountainhead belief is just too murky to understand, you can work backwards from the more accessible lesser heart beliefs that radiate from it. For example, if I am aware that my tribe does not trust anyone, but the reason for that is hidden from me, I would begin my search by breaking the vows holding that heart belief in place and start my investigation by asking questions of the Lord. Why is it that we cannot trust? What happened? Because heart beliefs are linked together you can work backwards by dismantling the lesser heart beliefs as they surface, while keeping an eye out for the fountainhead belief.

During your cleanse you will encounter spiritual realities such as agreements (bargains, deals, contracts, and covenants), unresolved ancestral emotions, judgments, empowered evil spirits, ancestral spirits, demonic trades, unanswered accusations, and so on. I discuss these in later chapters. Many of these kinds of problems resolve as you resolve the tribe's heart beliefs. Keep the tribe's heart at the forefront, and I will help you with the other.

Why Reconcile?

As the tribes of the earth responded to the challenges of the fall, their hearts became filled with wrong beliefs. These painful beliefs severed the tribes from their God-given identities and the gifts inherent within those identities. This did not happen because God withdrew their identities or the gifts, but because they saw themselves through a murky lens of rejection and resentment. It is time to repent. Repentance clears the way to accomplishing reconciliation with that gift-filled, glorious and fulfilling God-designed tribal identity. This restoration results in a reconciliation within relationships, both within and without the tribe, to the promised abundant life, and most of all to the One who created us for the sheer joy of it — God.

Why do I need to repent for what my ancestors believed?

The reason we need to repent for our inherited tribal heart beliefs is because at some point we agreed with what our tribe believes. When I could not have a pet baby alligator, I agreed with my ancestors. When I viewed everyone with suspicion, I was agreeing with my ancestors. I am no better than my mother or father or any person in my tribe. We all need to repent for believing in and agreeing with the lies that we have inherited.

How to repent

Repentance is best accomplished at the Cross of Christ. I suggest that you visualize being there as you work through the following steps. Don't worry if you can't visualize this; accept by faith that the Lord has taken you there.

1. The first step is to **accept** your tribe. This is easier for some. For others like me it is a struggle. Involve the Lord by engaging in a deep and honest conversation about all the reasons you wish He had made a different choice for you. Ask Him to explain why He made the choice He did. Be willing to accept your tribe even if you do not understand why God chose it for you. As you work on restoring your tribe you will discover the glory hidden underneath all the suffering. Discovering the glory makes it clear why God made the choice He made. Accepting your tribe is the first step toward being reconciled to your true tribal identity.

2. Once you have accepted your tribe (even if you are just in the process of that), **repent** for rejecting it. This is a personal repentance and must be done if you are going to represent the tribe.

    Repent like this:

    Lord God, I repent for rejecting my tribe. You chose this bloodline for me so I was rebelling against You when I rejected it. I ask for forgiveness. I ask Jesus to activate the words I have just spoken through the power of His blood.

    Again, I have found that this work is best done at the Cross.

3. **Identity:** Now you are positioned to represent your tribe. Start by repenting on behalf of the tribe for rejecting its God-given identity. Rejection always involves a condemning judgment. This means that the tribe passed judgment on itself, condemned itself, and started a process of attempting to reinvent itself. Do you see the rebellion against God that is inherent in that?

Repent like this:

I repent on behalf of myself and my people for believing the lie that our God-given identity is a bad thing. I repent for condemning that identity and for attempting to improve on what God made by inventing a new and improved identity. I ask Jesus to activate the words of repentance I have just spoken through the power of His blood and to turn me around into a new way.

4. **Relationship:** As you work through repentance it is a good idea to ask the Lord to show you what your tribe believes about others within and without the tribe. If you do not yet know the exact heart beliefs, rest assured that the tribe did believe lies about others and repent in a general way. You can polish up your repentance with specifics as you learn what they are.

    Repent like this:

    On behalf of myself and my tribe, I repent for the lies we believed about other people outside the tribe and within the tribe. I repent for judging and rejecting the men and/or the women and/or the children. I repent for judging outsiders and hurting them or rejecting them. Again I ask Jesus to activate the words of repentance I have just spoken through the power of His blood and to turn me around into a new way.

5. **Life:** One of saddest things we do is judge and reject life. When a tribe decides to believe that life is hurtful in some way, that tribe cannot receive the abundant life that Christ died to give it (John 10:10).

    Repent like this:

    On behalf of myself and my tribe, I repent for judging life, condemning it as bad and hurtful and rejecting it. I ask Jesus to empower the words of repentance I have just spoken at His Cross and to turn me around into His way. I ask for help receiving the abundant life He intends for me and my people to enjoy.

6. **God:** Blaming God for the bad things that happen within our fallen world is universal. Adam got that ball rolling when he condemned God with these words:

   "The woman whom You gave to be with me, she gave me fruit of the tree, and I ate."

   Genesis 3:12 ESV

   Repent like this:

   On behalf of myself and my tribe, I repent for blaming our suffering on You and choosing to believe that You are either indifferent to our suffering, cause us to suffer, or that You want us to suffer. I repent for turning away from You and rejecting the design, identity, purpose, and gifts You bestowed upon us. Once again, I ask Jesus to empower the words of repentance I have just spoken at His Cross and to turn me around into Your way.

7. **Sin:** The sinful actions that resulted because of the tribe's wrong heart beliefs hurt the tribe and those outside the tribe.

   Repent like this:

   I repent for the harm that we did to ourselves and others because of the lies we believed and I ask Jesus, through His blood, to empower these words. Please forgive us.

   How much better it is to get wisdom than gold! And to get understanding is to be chosen above silver.

   Proverbs 16:16

There are debts

Debts accrued by the tribe as it sinned its way through time must be paid. These debts are owed to every person the tribe hurt and to all of creation that was damaged by the tribe's actions. It is absolutely impossible for the tribe to pay off these debts. This inability to make things right opens the door to unrelenting guilt, shame, and regret. Until you know that the unpaid debts are paid you cannot escape being haunted by regret (Matthew 18:34). They must be paid and only the sacrifice of Christ can satisfy the demands of these debts.

You are already at the Cross, so ask the Lord Jesus to pay all debts owed by your tribe. Then ask Him to help you believe that His sacrifice is enough to settle your debts. Do not continue to try to pay them yourself. It is pointless. Honor Christ by accepting His sacrifice as the complete and eternal compensation for your personal debts and for those owed by your tribe. He will make right what you and your tribe have made wrong.

> *Having canceled the charge of our legal indebtedness, which stood against us and condemned us; He has taken it away, nailing it to the Cross.*
>
> Colossians 2:14 NIV

Pray like this:

> *Because we believed lies and responded in wrong ways, we have damaged our relationship with You, Lord. We have hurt ourselves, our children, and we have hurt other tribes. Please forgive us and please pay any debts that we owe.*

Healing and Restoration

Once repentance is offered to the Lord, ask Him to heal the tribal wounds and to restore your tribe's identity.

Pray like this:

> *Because we have believed lies, we have sinned. Because we have sinned, we are wounded. Please heal our wounds. And please restore our tribal identity. You have given us the responsibility of showcasing and releasing an important aspect of Your being and of Your heaven. We abandoned that responsibility when we rejected You and our identity. Now that I have repented for myself and my ancestors, I ask that You restore my tribe to its original purpose and design so that we can partner with You bringing Your will and kingdom into the earth.*

You will find as you are discovering and dismantling heart beliefs that repentance and reconciliation fits right into your restoration work. I suggest that you weave repentance and reconciliation prayers into the process, moving by the Spirit from your timeline to the Cross and back again.

Let's pray:

> *Our Father who is in heaven, hallowed be Your name. Your kingdom come. Your will be done, on earth as it is in heaven.*
>
> Matthew 6:9–10

Practice

1. Visualize standing at the Cross, if you can. If that's not possible, accept by faith that God will place you there. Choose to accept your tribe. Repent for rejecting it. Take note of what you see and sense. Repeat this exercise, taking your impressions and conflicts to the Lord, until you know that you have accepted your place as a tribal member.

2. Visualize standing at the Cross, if you can. Ask the Lord to pay all debts you and your people owe. Give Him your regret in exchange. Next, ask Him to pay all debts that are owed to you and your tribe. Repeat until you have a deep assurance that all debts have been zeroed out.

3. Ask the Lord to bring to mind the times you have blamed God for a confusing or painful circumstance. Discuss your feelings with Him and ask Him to help you understand. Do not answer the questions yourself. Wait for the Lord to answer.

CHAPTER 13

WONDERS, TERRORS, AND TREASURES

As I looked at the living creatures, I saw a wheel on the ground beside each creature with its four faces. This was the appearance and structure of the wheels: They sparkled like topaz, and all four looked alike. Each appeared to be made like a wheel intersecting a wheel. As they moved, they would go in any one of the four directions the creatures faced; the wheels did not change direction as the creatures went. Their rims were high and awesome, and all four rims were full of eyes all around.

Ezekiel 1:15–18 NIV

EZEKIEL'S VISION WAS FULL OF WONDERS, terrors, and treasures. You can expect much the same whenever you conduct a generational restoration. You will see marvelous and sometimes terrible things that will make you wonder. This is the nature of working within the spiritual realm.

I want to take a moment to look at the wheels that Ezekiel saw in the vision he was given. Notice that they were designed to go in every direction and that they were covered with eyes. If we consider the vision to be a symbolic representation of heaven, what do the wheels represent? They can go anywhere and they are all seeing. Both attributes suggest the omnipresence of God. He is everywhere and He sees all things. Ezekiel was seeing a picture of this aspect of our God. Are there really omni-directional wheels covered with eyes in heaven? Maybe, but what was much more important to the prophet Ezekiel was knowing that His all-knowing God was with Him wherever he went.

As you continue your cleanse, I want you to keep this in mind. What you discern needs to be considered from the symbolic angle first. What do these things represent? There are times when the Lord will reveal a literal circumstance to you. But run everything you discern through the symbolic angle first. Only then, should you consider if what you are discerning is a literal representation of what your tribe experienced.

Let's take stock of where you are in your generational restoration. You have stood at the beginning of your timeline, holding the restoration blessing that the Lord gave you when you were in the high court. You rolled that blessing down the first 500 years of your tribe's history, looking for the foundational heart belief. If you located that first heart belief, then you stepped down to that place on your timeline. You asked questions about the heart beliefs, broke vows, sent away spirits, and repented. You asked the Lord to pay the debts owed by your people and you asked for healing and reconciliation. Once you have, to the best of your knowledge, cleaned up that foundational belief, it is time to gather up the restoration blessing and send it further down your timeline. You are looking for lesser heart beliefs and the sin that resulted from your tribe's attempts at pain management.

If you did not find that first heart belief, or if you are just not sure about it, then gather up the blessing and send it down the timeline in search of the lesser heart beliefs. These lesser heart beliefs radiate from the foundational belief. The pattern of sin that you discover will also help identify what your tribe first believed within its tribal heart.

Moving Down The Timeline

Now that you have gathered up your restoration blessing, send it down the timeline another 500 years. Stop whenever you encounter a bump, roadblock, ditch, or pit. Explore the area around the barrier and begin the process of asking the Lord questions. Ask what happened? Why is there a blockage here? Also pay attention to the road or path that symbolizes your timeline. What does it look like? What does the landscape look like? Keep your senses engaged and stay alert to what you feel. Emotions are a primary way that we discern spiritual realities. If you begin to feel overwhelmed, ask the Lord what you are discerning about this tribe. Why does the tribe feel overwhelmed? What does the tribe believe that is resulting in such big emotions? Look and listen for pictures that symbolize the tribe's belief system.

If you still have not discovered the foundational belief, stay at the head of your timeline and send the restoration blessing down another 100 years or so. Repeat until a pattern of sin and lesser heart beliefs begin to assemble a picture of the tribe's foundational belief. Once that picture emerges, gather your blessing and resend it down the timeline looking for the moment in history when the tribe settled into its fountainhead heart belief.

As the Lord reveals the beliefs and sins of your people, do the work described in earlier chapters. One way that you can measure your progress is by how the larger spiritual picture changes. If the barrier clears and the landscape improves then the work you are doing is cleaning up the heart beliefs, sins, and traumas. For those of us who do not see very clearly, you may discern a lifting of strong negative emotion or a lightening of the atmosphere. Either way, once the work is done you will feel or receive a release to move forward. When you receive that release, gather up your restoration blessing, and send it further down the timeline. Continue this process until you reach the end of your timeline. At that point, extend the blessing to all your living relatives, both natural and spiritual, and send the blessing forward until the day Jesus returns.

Like this:

> *Through the name and the power of the blood and the Cross of Jesus, I ask Him to extend the cleansing and blessing to my immediate family, my extended family, and all my living relatives, spiritual and natural. I send it forward to the day that Jesus returns.*

Time Increments

When you begin the restoration, you are looking for that foundational heart belief which will have been established within the first 500 years of the tribe's history. Actually, it will most likely will have been established much sooner. So, you may want to begin with 100 years or even 50. How far down the timeline you send a restoration blessing is not set in stone. Any number of years that feels right to you is fine. Sometimes that means you only move in 50-year increments. Sometimes you will leap down 500 years. There will be times when you realize that you have missed something and need to turn around and go back. It is not unusual to go all the way back to the beginning of a timeline and start over.

The structure I have outlined for a generational restoration is just that — a structure. It helps contain some of the confusion that is inevitable when exploring a lost history by spiritual discernment. It also helps you be thorough. If you are just spot cleaning a problem area, it is pretty much inevitable that you will miss something important. Still, please do not be a slave to the structure. Use it to help you.

The Restoration Blessing

The restoration blessing you receive in the high court is symbolic of what your tribe lost because of its wrong heart beliefs. It is likely that you will not completely understand the meaning of the objects within the blessing. As the cleanse continues, the meaning within the blessing becomes clearer. Sometimes, that package of goodness is added to or even changed as you go along.

Sticking To The Timeline

It is perfectly fine to move from the timeline to the Cross for repentance work. You may find yourself prompted to return to the high court. Returning to the high court for help or clarification or just to get your bearings is perfectly acceptable.

The Lord is for me; I will not fear.

Psalm 118:6

When it is a big sin

I am often asked about big generational sins such as blood sacrifices and covenants, Satanic worship and witchcraft, child predation, and Masonic and cult involvement. Certain sins do open the door wider to the kingdom of darkness. So I understand the concern. And yes, please do repent for the sin. But keep your focus on WHY the tribe did what it did. I have never worked with a tribe involved in the Masonic that did not believe within its heart that it was weak and without honor. The Masonic promises protection, belonging, and honor within the community. If a tribe believes that it is vulnerable and without honor, those promises are very enticing. My paternal tribe became predators because they believed they could never have what they wanted the most. The sin always follows the belief.

> *When the woman saw that the tree was good for food, and that it was a delight to the eyes, and that the tree was desirable to make one wise, she took some of its fruit and ate.*
>
> Genesis 3:6

Eve believed that eating the fruit was the smart thing to do. She believed the lie first, then she sinned. Her action set the pattern for all humanity. First we believe, then we act. Adam responded in two ways: He went along to get along, and he chose his wife over God. Both of his decisions put in place patterns that affect how all of us struggle when faced with difficult choices.

It is essential that you resolve the underlying heart belief as you repent for the sin. This applies to all sin, big or small. The heart belief is the root of the tree that brings forth sin. Uproot the tree and sin dies.

Wonders You May Encounter

Setting aside heart beliefs for a moment, I want to familiarize you with some of the spiritual realities you may encounter as you conduct a cleanse. This overview is limited to my experiences so it is by no means comprehensive. Still, it is my hope that my experiences will prove to be useful to you.

Some sample prayers addressing the following issues are found in Chapter 16.

Portals

Certain kinds of agreements and/or sins open portals between our natural realm and the evil spiritual realm. These portals, or doorways, give access to dangerous spirits. Some portals, perhaps most, are opened unintentionally, but there are others that are opened on purpose.

The first time I encountered a portal while conducting a restoration I discerned it as an inverted tornado touching the land. All kinds of evil and chaos were spewing out of it. Please take note that I did not see it as a doorway. I saw a symbolic representation of an opening between the demonic and natural realm. Now you may discern a portal as a doorway. Then again, the doorway that you discern may not represent a portal. Do your best to avoid jumping to conclusions and seek interpretation from the Holy Spirit.

I honestly do not remember what the sin was that created the portal I discerned and it really does not matter. If you encounter an unholy portal, immediately stop your cleanse and ask the Holy Spirit HOW to repent for your people. Then follow the instructions that you are given. As you repent for the beliefs and actions that led to the opening of the portal, keep a watch on it. Keep working until you know that the portal has been closed.

I have encountered two other kinds of portals that had been opened in the past. Both were opened intentionally and both were located on another continent. I was attending church with a friend who was on the church's prayer team. She was concerned about a woman the team was continually praying for without any success. All their efforts at deliverance had failed. She told me that the woman often came to church dressed in skin-tight clothes and swayed about like a snake. That service this person arrived dressed in tight snakelike pants and carrying about her a sinuous quality. As I watched her the Holy Spirit told me that she was attached to a portal in Africa. In order for deliverance to be successful, she had to be released and the portal closed. This kind of portal is opened intentionally by a tribe seeking power from the demonic realm.

In a similar case, a man came to me asking for deliverance. Since early childhood he had been tormented by intrusions and visions of evil spirits. All his efforts to achieve freedom had failed. As we conducted a generational, we discovered that his tribe had covenanted with another tribe to open and maintain a portal to the demonic world. A boy child was selected from his tribe to sit within that portal and act as a go-between the spiritual and natural realm.

These days, the tribes have scattered and the agreement has been forgotten, but the spiritual enemy has not forgotten because the covenant was established in perpetuity and the portal was still open. The demonic realm was pushing spirits through this man whom it had chosen to sit within the portal that his ancestors had opened so many years ago.

In cases such as these, all deliverance efforts fail until the portal is closed and the person separated from it. This is because another spirit comes through the portal and replaces the one being cast out.

I am sure that there are other kinds of portals that you may encounter as you restore your bloodline. Unholy portals must be closed. Seek the direction of the Holy Spirit and continue to work on closing any portal until you know that it is complete. He will guide you. AND always ask what the tribe believed that led to it opening a portal. Cleanse the heart belief, break the vows, renounce any attached spirits, and instruct the tribal heart.

Not all portals will present as an inverted tornado. Also, there are holy and clean portals that bring God's goodness into the earth. These kinds of portals are blessings. If you find one of these treasures on your timeline, ask the Lord if the portal is the result of your tribe's good choices. Ask Him if you may reap the benefits of those good choices.

I cannot tell you how God will choose to show you any evil or holy portals. I can only encourage you to be on the lookout for them as you conduct your generational restoration.

Land

There are a number of issues with land that you may encounter as you cleanse. Defilement of land is not uncommon when certain kinds of violent or occult sins are committed on it. Trauma is one way unresolved emotions contaminate land. When a tribe is strongly bonded to land and then loses that land, if it does not willingly let go by choosing to go forward, the tribe may become stuck to the land even if they are living far from it. This is common among African American people who were forcibly removed from their land. The longing for that lost land lingers in their tribal heart which usually believes that there is no recovery because of this loss. I have not worked with Native Americans, but I would not be surprised if this kind of wound and heart belief is also common among them. This kind of connection is a trauma bond to land.

I worked with a person whose tribe during ancient times lost their land to a warlike tribe. They were grief-stricken, but managed to avoid blaming God until another traumatic loss occurred. At that point, they became convinced that they could not recover from their losses. The tribe turned on God, vowing to never trust Him again. Their descendants now struggle with a compulsory rage directed at God. This rage overflows during difficult times. Because the real reason for the rage is lost in time, the descendants focus on whatever challenge is in front of them.

When the Holy Spirit draws your attention to the condition of the land and to the tribe's relationship to it, look for these three issues: defilement, ancestral emotions, and trauma bonds. Ask how to pray in order to release the tribe and to bring cleansing and healing to the land.

Time

Like land, time (and even the atmosphere) may be defiled by sin or trauma. A tribe may become stuck in time so that it is unable to move into the present. Much like a tribe traumatically bonded to land, a tribe may be bonded to a traumatic event in its past or even bonded to one wonderful time that the tribe is unwilling to give up. When a tribe is unwilling to live in the present, evil spirits remove the tribe's perception of reality and create an illusion for the tribe to live within. As I am sure you can imagine, a tribe stuck in the past cannot prosper.

When trauma repeats year after year at the same time, there is a strong possibility that the tribe is bonded to a traumatic event in the past. Search out the heart beliefs about time and what the tribe believes will happen *every time.*

Objects

I have not experienced this very much but others whom I respect report it so I am including it in the event that you find it on the timeline. Remove any bonds to objects such as altars, devices, and clothing that were used for unholy ceremonies by renouncing the ceremonies and asking the Holy Spirit to disconnect the tribe from those things.

Graves

It is possible for a tribe or tribe member to be bound to a grave or to the place where traumatic death occurred. It is also possible that ceremonies were conducted that bound members of the tribe to gravesites. Look for the underlying beliefs that caused the tribe to cling to graves, gravesites, or sites of traumatic death.

But what if it is literal?

Now a word of caution here. Seeing graves or gravesites or altars and ceremonial objects does not automatically mean anything literal. They may be symbols. So, seek interpretation before leaning into a possible literal meaning. But know that God will reveal actual historical facts to you if they are relevant. You may see a vision of the tribe being forced off its land. You may see a vision of a drought, famine, plague, or battle. These probably actually happened. One instance that I never understood if it was literal or symbolic was a reoccurring vision of a woman trapped in a cave, weeping her heart out. Did that really happen or did she represent the trauma the women of the tribe suffered? When I was cleansing my maternal tribe, I saw a vision of a man on a boat flinging a woman overboard. I do not know if that really happened or if it represents the tribal heart belief that women are expendable. Ultimately, what matters most is discovering the underlying heart belief being exposed through visions.

Here is an interesting experience I had when working with a family struggling with inherited mental illness. During a generational cleanse, the Lord showed me an ancestor who served by day as a Catholic priest and by night as a priest of Satan. He used the sacred vessels in his satanic worship. This opened a door to the demonic on the bloodline. The Lord revealed this historical fact in a vision. It was as if I was watching a movie. And to this day I am convinced that I was seeing what actually had happened.

Agreements

I am grouping all agreements together. These are the covenants, bargains, deals, and contracts entered into, knowingly or unknowingly, with evil forces by the tribe or the tribe's representatives. Agreements made with the demonic always involve a trade of some kind. These trades may be considered temporary on the side of humans, but they are considered permanent on the side of the demonic. I will go into more detail about trades in Chapter 15.

Agreements are best annulled by the blood of Jesus and in the high court of heaven or another heavenly court that the Lord directs you to. There is much written and taught on courts of heaven intercession. I will not tackle that topic in this book other than to provide some guidance in Chapter 15. Just know that these kinds of agreements are legal constructs, so dismantling them in God's courts is an effective approach.

Be on the lookout for any agreement with death. Such an agreement is fairly common and is usually made unknowingly when the tribe decides that it should never have been created and that death is a desirable escape from its pain. This kind of agreement empowers a spirit of death to prey upon the people. Remember to discover the underlying heart belief. Clean that up, then renounce the agreement. I will offer more guidance on how to accomplish this in Chapter 16.

> *Just say a simple, 'Yes, I will,' or 'No, I won't.' Anything beyond this is from the evil one.*
>
> Matthew 5:37 NLT

Ancestral spirits

African, Asian, and Native American people understand that the spirits of ancestors do not necessarily leave the earth realm when they die. I have worked with the descendants of African tribes that intentionally held onto their ancestors after death, one tribe going so far as to embed the human spirit of a revered leader within a child chosen to embody it. Although the practice of clinging to ancestral spirits may no longer be carried out, the spirits that were held onto continue down the generational line until directed elsewhere.

Whenever there is ancestor worship, there is a high likelihood that the human spirits of the dead will still be with us, often attached to their descendants.

When working with a former member of the Jehovah Witnesses, she told me that she discerned a number of deceased family members — also Witnesses — that hung around her because they believed that they were not acceptable to God. Because she was invested herself in being quiet and hiding, these human spirits felt safe hiding with her.

This kind of lingering after death is not uncommon when the death is unexpected and traumatic. Or when the person has nowhere to go because they do not believe that God wants them. Stories of battlefields haunted by those who died there are not uncommon. Once, I was invited to the birthday party of a physician. Unbeknownst to me, he was an abortionist and those who worked for him were in attendance. This happened before I had been introduced to the idea of lingering human spirits. I kept feeling the presence of babies in the atmosphere. Eventually, I realized that I was discerning the spirits of the aborted who believed they had nowhere to go so they clung to those who had aborted them.

Ancestral emotions

Not only do unresolved emotions contaminate land, time, and atmosphere, big unresolved emotions may be transferred onto the next generation, often through abuse. This happens when the tribe does not know how to resolve their emotions. Usually there is a heart belief that there is nothing that can be done and that there is no recovery. So downloading the emotional overload into children or other vulnerable tribe members becomes the tribe's coping mechanism. A clean-up prayer is found in Chapter 16, but be aware as you move down the timeline that pockets of emotion belonging to those who are long dead may be discovered. Ask the Lord to remove these emotions from the timeline and also from any living person who is carrying emotions that are not their own.

Recall the tribe that was so enraged with God because of their losses. This unmanageable emotion was downloaded into the children through abuse and neglect. But unresolved generationally based emotions may also be transferred in other ways. As mother and father engage with the children, they communicate through eye contact, actions, and words what they believe about who they are as a people.

Common kinds of evil spirits

I am going to limit this discussion to three high-level evil spirits. This triad, or tripod as one of my ministry team members calls it, works together. Other spirits may be present, of course, but these three are almost always present and they actively work against any effort made to restore a tribe. Most of the other spirits you may come across will either be working with these three or will be able to do their dirty work because of these three big hitters. Each of these three spirits tampers with our natural senses so that we do not perceive or recognize the truth.

The deaf and dumb spirit

This spirit activates whenever the tribe vows to do whatever it takes to keep what it believes and what happened secret. I have seen it in a vision looking like a long thick worm laying across the timeline, allegedly there to help the tribe keep its secrets but, in reality, it is preventing the tribe from recovering.

I have only seen the deaf and dumb spirit a few times. I usually discern it by yawning uncontrollably. Sometimes I will want to cover my face with my hands. This spirit more than any other hides secrets. When you discern it, or if you are still struggling to get insights after you have broken the blocking vows, consider the possibility that you are being opposed by a deaf and dumb spirit.

I begin the process of removing it by asking what the secret is. I want to know what the tribe believes that it is desperately trying to hide. Once, you get some idea of the possible secret — it will usually be something along the lines of *we are disgusting, we are unlovable, we are the rejected, we are evil, we are weak, we are foolish* — apply what you have learned about removing heart beliefs. Because the deaf and dumb spirit is a high-level fallen being, ask the Lord to remove it for you once you have finished the heart work.

Another high-level being that will work beside the deaf and dumb spirit is the spirit of forgetting. The spirit of forgetting affects memory and rewrites history. Ask the Lord to remove this from your bloodline once you have finished working on the heart beliefs that invited it in.

The spirit of unbelief

The second leg of our triad is the spirit of unbelief. Rather than cause a tribe to disbelieve God — that is one role of the spirit of forgetting which causes us to forget all the times God has helped us — this spirit causes us to disbelieve our own senses. Under its influence, we doubt what we see and hear and even know.

Unbelief works alongside the deaf and dumb spirit by making what the tribe believes about itself inscrutable. It does this by twisting the perception of reality so that outsiders misperceive the tribe. You may have experienced the influence of unbelief in the workplace or in the church. The leader is obviously corrupt, but everyone is second-guessing themselves because they distrust their own senses.

If you begin to discern a lot of confusion and misdirection on the bloodline, and if you begin to distrust what you are discerning, ask the Lord if a spirit of unbelief is operating. As you dismantle the belief system hidden under vows of secrecy, this spirit is powered down. Ask the Lord to remove it once the heart work is finished.

The spirit of control (slavery)

The third leg of this secrecy triad is the spirit of control. Many believers know this best as the spirit of religion, but it is actually a spirit of control or slavery. Heavy-handed religion is only one way that it manifests. Within a generational, this spirit works alongside the deaf and dumb and unbelief spirits to control and manipulate the flow of information about the tribe. It does this by attempting to control what we perceive and how we perceive it. This works against outsiders recognizing the truth, but for those within the tribe it works to keep the secrets hidden and the belief system in place. It often does this by calling the spirit of abuse alongside to punish any tribe member that does not keep the secrets or agree with the tribal heart beliefs.

When I have seen this spirit, it looks like a spinning octopus, its many legs reaching out to control. I have seen this spirit during generationals, but I have also seen it sitting on top of governmental buildings and on top of individuals.

Begin to remove the spirit of control by addressing the tribe's belief that truth and reality are enemies and that exposure will result in death by shame. Repent for participating in mind control and abuse. Ask the

Lord to remove it once the heart beliefs are dismantled and repentance is complete.

Generational Blessings

There was a tribe that made a terrible decision to abandon children because there was not enough food. The Lord showed us that one woman refused to agree with the tribe's decision and remained behind with the children. She was willing to die with them rather than abandon them. Her choice left a huge blessing on the timeline that was available to any tribe member who had decided to follow Jesus despite the cost. These kinds of blessings may appear as clean running water, an oasis, a snow bank, a bubbling fountain, or other refreshing image. Be on the lookout for hidden pockets of blessings and buried treasure. When you run across such blessings, ask the Lord to release them to you.

The Tribal Gift

Every tribe is designed to carry and release some aspect of God's goodness and character in the earth. These tribal gifts are never removed by God, but they have become twisted or buried because they were targeted by the enemy who does not want any aspect of our Creator expressed. As you remove the wrong heart beliefs, vows, and attached spirits, your tribal gifting will become more obvious.

Often the foundational heart belief is the opposite of the tribe's gift. In the case of my paternal tribe, it carries and is capable of expressing Father God's love through provision. The opposite of that is believing that Father God withholds His provision because He does not love us. As you search for the gift woven into a tribe's design, consider the flip side of the foundational heart belief. And, of course, always ask the Holy Spirit to reveal the tribal gift.

Once the tribal gift is restored you will walk in it by simply being you. No action is required to activate the gift. It is woven into your very design.

Let's pray:

> *There is a lot here, Lord. More than I can ever remember. Please bring to my mind what I need to recall as I work to restore my generational line or help others. Help me remember to consider everything I discern as symbolic. And help me to know when what You are revealing is not symbolic but a historical event. Teach me to lean on You.*
>
> *In Jesus' name. Amen*
>
> *There are more things in heaven and earth, Horatio, than are dreamt of in your philosophy.*

From Shakespeare's *Hamlet*

Practice

1. Practice moving from the timeline, to the Cross, to the high court, and back to the timeline. Describe or sketch how each of those places look and feel to you.

2. Imagine standing before the high court and asking that the record of tribal agreements be opened. Think about the sin patterns in your family line. What might be written in that record?

3. Practice moving your restoration blessing down the timeline in different increments. Move it down 50 years, 100 years, and 500 years. Ask the Holy Spirit to show you how many years to move the blessing each time you send it down.

4. The tribal gift is often the opposite of the foundational heart belief. If you know the foundational heart belief of your tribe, ask the Lord if the opposite of the heart belief is the tribe's gift.

CHAPTER 14

THE BLAME GAME

And He said, "Who told you that you were naked? Have you eaten from the tree from which I commanded you not to eat?"
The man said, "The woman whom You gave to be with me, she gave me some of the fruit of the tree, and I ate."

Genesis 3:11–12

Blaming and Blame Shifting

THERE IS A CHAPTER IN John Sandford's book *The Renewal of the Mind*[12] titled *"Roots and Ruts Devolved from Adam and Eve's Sinful Replies to God in the Garden of Eden."* That is a mouthful, isn't it? Sandford discusses

---

12   John L. Sandford and R. Loren Sandford, *The Renewal of the Mind*, (Victory House, Inc., 1991), 119.

how we, as descendants of Adam and Eve, come into the world already programmed to respond just like they did. This means that we are prone to blame the wrong thing and blame shift whenever faced with difficulties. Now, as far as a generational restoration is concerned blaming is a huge issue. Tribes often will blame other groups within the tribe. The men blame the women and vice versa. The old people may be blamed and so might the young. This blaming allows room for spirits of abuse and neglect to run rampant through the tribe. After all, if it is the women's fault or the men's fault then abusing them feels justified. They deserve to be punished. As you conduct your cleanse, keep a lookout for the blaming of any sub-group within the tribe. My maternal tribe is a good example of this. The tribe believed within its heart that the women were expendable. Since the tribe believed the women had no value, abusing and neglecting them was acceptable.

As you break the vows holding any heart beliefs in place, repent for blaming the wrong thing or the wrong people. The real reason that bad things happen is because of the fall. That is the only reason bad things happen. If you do not believe me, give it some thought. That is what I did. I wanted to believe that my bad decisions or the bad decisions of others were causing all the bad things, but when I looked behind those bad decisions, I found the fallen state of humanity. For the tribal heart or, for that matter, the personal heart, telling it to blame the fall for bad things is enough. It only needs to believe that bad things happen because of the fall.

As you break these kinds of vows always ask the Lord what other vows surround the one holding the heart belief in place.

There is another kind of blaming that is more subtle but also devastating. And that is when a tribe blames something good for causing something bad.

Misplaced blame

This tendency to blame something good was first illustrated to me while working with an African woman. She explained that child abuse, including sexual abuse, was common among her people. All of the adult family members abused the children and even forced some out of the family home at an early age. As we investigated her timeline, we discovered that the tribe blamed its innocence for causing a traumatic event. In ancient times, a predatory tribe had approached her people, offering friendship. When her tribe innocently offered friendship in return, it was attacked, the women raped, the men beaten and killed, and their possessions plundered.

The tribe blamed its innocence — if the people had been tough, smart, and cunning — they would not have been tricked. From that, the tribe formed this heart belief: *Innocence is bad. It makes terrible things happen.* It decided to never be innocent again, vowing to become smart, tough, and cunning. It then became imperative to stop protecting the innocence of the children. Instead, the tribe worked together to destroy it. Tribe members believed that they are keeping the children safe from being tricked.

Here are a few of the God-given good things and perfect gifts that are blamed when bad things happen. This is not a comprehensive list.

> Trust — Trust caused the bad thing to happen.
> *We will never trust again.*
>
> Joy — If we had not been joyful (happy), then the bad thing would not have happened. *We will never be joyful again.*
>
> Gentleness — We were hurt because we were gentle.
> *We will never be gentle again.*
>
> Kindness — Kindness made the bad thing happen.
> *We will never be kind again.*

Hope — If we had not hoped, then we would not have been disappointed. *We will never hope again.*

Love — Our love hurt us. *We will never love again.*

Every good thing given and every perfect gift is from above, coming down from the Father of lights ...

James 1:17

Everything on my list is a God quality. When we blame the qualities and characteristics of God, we are blaming God, usually inadvertently. Though some tribes do blame God directly.

As you cleanse, ask the Lord to show you what the tribe blamed for the traumas. Repent for blaming the wrong thing and direct the tribal heart to understand the fall as the source of suffering instead.

Like this:

Heart, you will no longer blame the wrong thing. (Just fill in the blank with what the tribe has blamed). You will understand instead that suffering comes from the fall. The fall is the reason that bad things happen. It is the only reason and that is all you need to understand. You will allow God to teach us to trust, love etc. (Fill in with what the tribe blamed). You will not push Him away.

You will need to repent of the heart beliefs, break the vows, and send the spirits away. Ask the Lord to restore your tribe's ability to flow in whatever good and perfect gift that was blamed.

Two kinds of judgment

"Do not judge so that you will not be judged. For in the way you judge, you will be judged ..."

Matthew 7:1–2

I would like to start this section by clearing up a common misunderstanding about the warning against judging. In the New Testament there are two Greek words that are translated into the English word *judge*. The word 'krino' is found in Matthew 7:1–2 and it means to *judge with condemnation*. This is the kind of judging Jesus warned about. When we judge with a condemning attitude, we reap condemning judgment. The other Greek word is 'anakrino'. Paul uses 'anakrino' in 1 Corinthians 2:15 when he explains that believers with the Holy Spirit are capable of discerning accurately, or judging, all things. The kind of judging that causes ruinous reaping is the topic of this section.

Shifting from Blame to Judgment to Rejection

Much 'krino' judgment happens without a tribe's conscious knowledge. Look at the list above and notice that the heart beliefs automatically shift from blaming to judging. For example, the tribe that believed being innocent was the cause of it being tricked quickly made the decision that innocence is bad. From that it was a short step to looking at innocence with contempt. Let me chart that for you.

The trauma happens and the tribe believes:

> We were tricked because we were innocent.
>
> Being innocent is stupid and dangerous — « THIS IS THE JUDGMENT
>
> We will do whatever it takes to never be innocent again.

At this point the tribe becomes compelled to eradicate innocence wherever it is found.

> ... I want you to be wise in what is good, and innocent in what is evil.
>
> Romans 16:19

Here are some other good things that a tribe may blame, judge, and reject.

Truth

When a tribe believes that a painful lie is the truth, it will believe that truth is causing pain. It may believe that knowing the truth is too shameful to endure. When this happens, a tribe will do whatever it takes to hide from the truth, saying within its heart that truth hurts. This will make it difficult for the tribe to be comfortable with Jesus since He is the truth.

> Jesus said, "I am the way, and the truth, and the life ..."
>
> John 14:6

Reality

Believing that reality is too harsh to bear is the reason a tribe turns away from reality and embraces an illusion. Jesus faced the reality of the Cross and in doing so paved the way for us to embrace reality no matter how painful it may be.

> Looking only to Jesus ... who for the joy set before Him endured the Cross, despising the shame, and has sat down at the right hand of the throne of God.
>
> Hebrews 12:2

Life

When a tribe decides that life itself is to blame for its suffering, it will blame, judge, and reject life. This opens the door for the tribe to turn to death as a means of escape from the pain of life. The tribe becomes unable to accept the abundant life that Jesus promised. The tribal heart actually pushes away the life God offers.

> *The thief comes only to steal and kill and destroy; I came so that they would have life, and have it abundantly.*
>
> John 10:10

The Tribal Gift

Because the tribal gift is woven into the very fabric of every tribe member, rejecting that gift means the tribe has rejected its God-given identity. Once that happens the tribe loses its purpose, confusion sets in, and the tribe becomes a wanderer in the earth.

> *They wandered in the wilderness in a desert region. They did not find a way to an inhabited city.*
>
> Psalm 107:4

Judging the Creator

When we judge any aspect of creation, we are judging the Creator. Even fallen spiritual beings, who were created by God, should not be judged by us. While blame may be placed upon these creatures for tempting the tribe into sin, shifting that blame into judgment causes the tribe to reap judgment. Only God has the right to judge with condemnation any part of His creation. Recall Jesus' warning that 'krino' judgment causes condemnation to be reaped. If I judge a fallen evil being for its actions, I must ask if I am guilty of those same actions. Have I tried to control others? Have I ever manipulated? Have I stolen? Have I ever used someone? Have I abused myself or anyone else? Have I lied for personal gain?

This does not mean that these beings are blameless, or that I should be unaware of their evil intent. It is appropriate to practice 'anakrino' judgment. But unless you are an unfallen being who has never sinned, it is better to leave 'krino' judgment in the hands of God.

At the root of all of this blaming, judging, and rejecting is anger at God the Creator. God is being blamed, judged, and rejected whenever we decide that one of His good and perfect gifts is the cause of our suffering. We are blaming and judging God whenever we accuse and condemn some aspect of His creation, including ourselves. That a tribe is holding God accountable for its suffering may be hidden, but oftentimes a tribe is openly hostile toward God.

As you discover what a tribe has blamed, judged, and rejected, be sure to repent for blaming, judging, and rejecting God.

Recovery

As you stand on your timeline, rolling the restoration blessing down the years, ask the Holy Spirit to show you who and what the tribe blamed, judged, and rejected as it struggled to manage the trauma of living in a fallen world.

I work on each thing that the tribe has blamed one at a time. If the tribe blamed joy, I work on cleaning that up. If the tribe also rejected its tribal gift, I clean that up next. Remember that any judgment against God's gifts, design, or creation automatically includes judgment against the Creator. So be sure to repent for that. Break the vows holding the heart beliefs in place. The judgments flow from what the tribal heart believes. Ask the Lord to rebuke and send away attached evil spirits and instruct the heart.

Like this:

> *Heart, the reason the bad thing happened is because of the fall. Joy did not cause it. The tribal gift did not cause it. God did not cause it. The fall caused it. From now on, you will understand that the bad thing is a result of the fall. You will allow the tribe to experience joy. You will allow the tribe to walk in its design. You will stop pushing God away. You will allow Him to bless me and my people with every good thing and perfect gift.*

Mistreatment By Other Tribes

> *I am surrounded by enemies, who are like lions hungry for human flesh.*
>
> Psalm 57:4 GNT

As the tribes scattered across the face of the earth, many began fighting with one another over land and resources. These battles often left smaller tribes decimated. More powerful tribes subjugated weaker ones, sometimes enslaving them or plundering their goods.

> *The Midianites were stronger than Israel, and the people of Israel hid from them in caves and other safe places in the hills. Whenever the Israelites would plant their crops, the Midianites would come with the Amalekites and the desert tribes and attack them. They would camp on the land and destroy the crops as far south as the area around Gaza. They would take all the sheep, cattle, and donkeys, and leave nothing for the Israelites to live on. They would come with their livestock and tents, as thick as locusts. They and their camels were too many to count. They came and devastated the land, and Israel was helpless against them.*
>
> Judges 6:2–6 GNT

I worked with an American man whose tribe had been crushed by another tribe and made to be its servant. His tribe suffered from extremely low self-worth. This sense of being without value was passed to the children.

Condemning judgments often result when a tribe is injured by another tribe. Because 'krino' judgment results in reaping judgment, you will find that the victim tribe has developed sinful behaviors that often mirror the tribe it judged. Sometimes, a victim tribe will vow to never be like its oppressor. In such cases, the tribe is sidelining its God-given identity in an effort to be the opposite of the oppressor. In either instance, until the victim tribe accepts that it is no better than its attackers and repents, the sinful behaviors will continue.

> *For all have sinned and fall short of the glory of God …*
>
> Romans 3:23

As you seek healing and freedom, repent for the condemning judgments. It is sometimes helpful to ask the Holy Spirit to show you how the victim tribe has behaved like the attacking tribe.

Here is a model strategic prayer.

> *Lord God, Your Son Jesus died for the sins of all humanity including those committed by my tribe and by the tribes that attacked and oppressed us. When my tribe judged another tribe, we were claiming to be superior to that tribe. We are not superior. We have sinned. We have hurt people. And we have dishonored You. I repent for the judgments we have made. And I ask that all the reaping from those judgments be directed to the Cross.*
>
> *In Jesus' name. Amen.*

If the tribe is a predator tribe (my paternal tribe was a predator), then repent for its sins and ask the Lord to pay all the debts the tribe owes to those it has hurt.

Let's pray:

> *Father God, Creator of all that is, I have sinned because I have blamed what is good. I have blamed others. I have blamed creation, and I have blamed You for my suffering and the suffering of my people. Please forgive us. Show me the judgments we have made so that I may repent. Teach me to leave 'krino' judgment in Your hands and give me the wisdom to judge with discernment and without condemnation.*
>
> *In Jesus' name. Amen.*

Practice

1. God says that He is love. What do you think might happen if a tribe blames love? Choose one of the other gifts from the list and write out a possible heart belief. Then think about vows the tribe might have made as they tried to manage that heart belief. How do you think the tribe treated their children? What would they teach them?

2. Ask the Holy Spirit if your tribe has blamed any good thing for its suffering. When He shows you, look for the underlying heart belief and the judgment that flows from it. What vow did your tribe make to manage what it believed? How has that borne fruit in your life?

CHAPTER 15

TRADES AND ACCUSATIONS

Through your widespread trade you were filled with violence, and you sinned. So I drove you in disgrace from the mount of God and I expelled you, guardian cherub, from among the fiery stones.

Ezekiel 28:16 NIV

I REMEMBER BEING VERY SURPRISED when I saw in Ezekiel 28:16 that Lucifer *aka* Satan, the guardian cherub, was engaged in some kind of questionable trade. I had been taught that pride was Satan's sin, and perhaps it was pride that led him to conduct these widespread trades. If you look at the passages in Isaiah 14 and Ezekiel 28, it seems very likely that Satan was planning a coup against God.

> *But you said in your heart,*
> *'I will ascend to heaven; I will raise my throne above the stars of God,*
> *And I will sit on the mount of assembly in the recesses of the north.*

> *I will ascend above the heights of the clouds; I will make myself like the Most High.'*
>
> Isaiah 14:13–14

Perhaps Satan was promising to give other celestial beings status and power within his regime in exchange for their help overthrowing God. That would be a trade. It is unclear exactly what Satan was up to with his trading, but we do know from Scripture that it resulted in filling him with violence and led him to sin.

Satan and other fallen celestial beings are still master traders. They eagerly offer humanity whatever we think we want in return for something that they can use to enslave us. For example, the Masonic cult offers protection, belonging, and honor to a tribe that believes it is vulnerable and despised. The question is: What do the spirits behind Freemasonry require in return? In brief, oaths are required and rituals conducted that bind a man's loyalty first and foremost to the lodge. This violates the first commandment. The oaths also include horrible consequences for violating this loyalty. Here are the consequences of just the first-degree of masonry.

> The obligation of a first-degree Freemason (Entered Apprentice degree):
>
> Binding myself under no less a penalty than that of having my throat cut across, my tongue torn out by its roots, and buried in the rough sands of the sea at low-water mark, where the tide ebbs and flows twice in twenty-four hours, should I ever knowingly or willingly violate this my solemn oath and obligation as an Entered Apprentice Mason. So help me God, and keep me steadfast in the due performance of the same.[13]

The lodge offers security in exchange for absolute loyalty. If that loyalty is violated, the enemy gets access to the family's health. Yes. I said

---

13   https://www.evangelicaltruth.com/freemasonry-oaths/

family. Within the spiritual realm, the man is automatically regarded as the representative of his bloodline. A woman entering into the oaths of the Order of the Eastern Star, the female version of Freemasonry, is considered the representative of her tribe. Thus, all the consequences of disloyalty fall upon any descendent who is not loyal to Freemasonry. On the surface, what has been traded is one's personal loyalty in exchange for honor, security, and belonging. But what is also being quietly traded is permission to devastate the health and well-being of every family member and descendent in perpetuity. That is a demonic trade.

Trade Representatives

No one becomes a Freemason except for personal gain. As you cleanse your generational line, be on the lookout for instances when your tribe became so invested in gaining some advantage that it was willing to make a trade. If you discover any kind of ritual or sacrifice, or just come across a bump in the road where you feel the need to ask questions, stop and ask the Lord what was the tribe seeking and what was it willing to trade.

Leaders can make demonic trades that affect their followers. King Mesha of Moab sacrificing his firstborn son to Chemosh is a good example of this. He traded the life of his heir for deliverance from the Israelites. After that trade was made, the evil being Chemosh had a spiritual right to demand access to all of the Moabites' firstborn sons. That celestial being had the right because the King represented all of his people.

> *When the king of Moab saw that the battle had gone against him, he took with him seven hundred swordsmen to break through to the king of Edom, but they failed. Then he took his firstborn son, who was to succeed him as king, and offered him as a sacrifice on the city wall. The fury against Israel was great; they withdrew and returned to their own land.*
>
> 2 Kings 3:26–27 NIV

Here is another case of a leadership trade that resulted in dismal consequences for the followers. I was part of a charismatic church that enjoyed successful deliverances, healings, and other supernatural experiences. But those manifestations of the Holy Spirit began to fall off during the early 1990s. At that time, a call to unity was the trendy thing amongst the Protestant churches. My pastor and the other pastors of the area's charismatic churches agreed to meet with the much more prominent, prosperous, and powerful leaders of the area's evangelical churches. The goal was to create unity between the denominations. There was only one requirement. The Holy Spirit had to be parked at the door. You see, signs and wonders, deliverance and healing, but most especially tongues, were not acceptable to the better educated evangelical pastors who were important community leaders. So sadly, the charismatic pastors abandoned what they knew to be true in exchange for acceptance and belonging. Oh, it was sugar-coated as a unity move, but it was really an ambitious bid for position.

What were the consequences of this demonic trade? Ambition that is willing to compromise opens the door to a high-level celestial being known as Python, the spirit of constriction. After the charismatic leaders traded the Holy Spirit in exchange for acceptance and a share of the glory enjoyed by the more respected evangelical pastors, Python gripped the churches in the area and forced conformity onto them. Conformity is an imitation of unity. It forces each individual to become the same by squeezing to death any unique expression.

As the years have passed, each individual church in my area — regardless of the denomination — has become the same. There is no life, freedom, or manifested presence of the Holy Spirit. The few nondenominational charismatic churches have dwindled down to a handful. One is weary and struggling, its leader devastated with ongoing health issues. Another that is located in an outlying area has not grown in years and years. The Assembly of God church is a Masonic stronghold and the Church of God … well, here is what happened when I visited.

In search of a church that my family and I could be a part of, I visited our community's Church of God. I was enjoying the congregation's enthusiastic worship when the Lord opened my eyes to a spiritual reality. In the spirit, I saw a huge upright snake slither into the sanctuary. As I watched it, the Lord informed me that it was making its Sunday rounds through all the area churches. As it passed through the church I was in, the atmosphere darkened, the people's mood flattened, and the worship became lifeless.

My family and I have watched the consequences of this trade relentlessly overtake all the churches as, one by one, any unique expression of God was smothered. As much as we would like to meet within the walls of the traditional church, we cannot. Instead, we meet with other trusted believers in our homes where there is no foothold for Python because there is no ambition. There is no ambition, not because we are exceptionally good people, but because we have agreed to take no offering, except to help one another if in need, and to appoint no pastor. We worship the Lord, we pray for one another, and we read the Word of God together. Then we eat.

The believers in my area are suffering because their representatives made a trade with the demonic. Do I think that the leaders knew what they were doing at the time? I think they knew that they were making a compromise, but I do not think they realized that they were trading with the demonic or what the consequences of that trade would be.

Our ancestors in all likelihood did not realize that their trades with the demonic had generational consequences. But all demonic trades have a hidden this-is-forever tag attached to them. It is our responsibility to get these trades overturned.

Overturning Demonic Trades

I am going to get into some courts of heaven protocols here, limiting this discussion to trades and accusations. Since I started with trades, I will lay out how I approach the high court of God for the purpose of overturning trades found during a generational restoration.

Steps to overturning trades

1. Approach the court whenever you discern that the tribe participated in a demonic trade. If you are familiar with courts of heaven intercession, you may want to have the generational line's records pulled so that you can examine them. If you find any trades that need to be overturned, you can have that taken care of in the appropriate court. But because the focus of this book is on generational issues and since we are already working within the high court, let's go there whenever a demonic trade is discovered on the timeline.

2. Respectfully ask the court to open the record books to the trade that you discovered. Ask if there is any impediment to overturning and canceling the trade. The court will explain what you need to do to have the trade canceled.

3. Follow the court's instructions which will include repentance for making the trade and repudiation of all benefits gained from the trade.

Here is a sample prayer for overturning trades. It is to be presented before the court.

> *As a representative of my bloodline, I repent for myself and my people for trading with the demonic. I repent for believing that such a trade was good and necessary. I repent for believing that You Lord God were not willing to help and for not turning to You. I ask Jesus to empower the words of repentance I have just spoken through His shed blood.*

I ask You, Lord, to forbid retaliation against me, my tribe, our friends and all we are given to steward as I now repudiate and reject all benefits gained from the trade. I ask Jesus to cancel and overturn the trade on the Cross. Please restore whatever was given away by my people. Please rebuke and cast out every evil spirit involved in this deceptive trade.

I ask for the blood of Jesus to witness on my behalf and on the behalf of my people. He died for our sins. His sacrifice is enough to pay the debts that we owe because of this trade.

Once you are satisfied that the trade has been overturned, return to the generational timeline and see what has changed. You will discern if your work in the courtroom has resolved the trade. Continue to work on the trade until you know that it has been canceled and restoration has been made.

Accusations

Our spiritual enemy is prowling around looking for someone to devour. One way that he is able to attack is through accusations. Now, these accusations do not have to be true or fair. They just need some human to be making them. The Lord taught me about accusations when I was in a struggle over my mother's will. A family member was enraged about how my mother decided to dispose of her assets and blamed me for those decisions. I was standing in my kitchen one day when I noticed that I was being bombarded in my mind with angry accusations about my integrity. The rage felt like a physical thing. As I leaned into this spiritual reality, the Lord revealed that this relative was breathing out accusations against me. He wanted me to be punished. An evil spirit had heard him and agreed to carry out his will by attacking me. I do not think that this relative was aware that evil spirits will partner with the accusations we make and punish those we are accusing.

Here is another example that might help explain this phenomenon. I was working with a woman who was a surprise baby. Her parents were disappointed to learn that they were having another child and her brother resented the new baby, feeling replaced. He blamed her for making everyone unhappy and ruining his life. He wanted her dead or at least to not exist. This accusation was picked up in the spirit and evil spirits were sent to punish the new child for existing.

When accusations go unchallenged, they continue down the generational line. My relative was accusing me of being a thief and my friend's brother was accusing her of ruining everything. These accusations would have passed down the bloodline if we had not challenged them.

When you are conducting your cleanse, be aware that any accusation leveled against the tribe is best answered in the courts of heaven. If the tribe is a predator tribe that mistreated others, then it is very likely that it has accusations lodged against it. If the tribe falls more into the victim category, it may have made accusations that empowered the demonic to bring about evil. And it also may have accusations against it. Remember that the accusations do not need to be accurate. Evil spirits just need humans to make them.

I want to be clear that God is not making these accusations and they are not being heard in one of His courts. These kinds of accusations are heard in the court of hell. A guilty verdict is decided there and a punishing sentence assigned to the accused.

How to Challenge Accusations

While you are cleansing, if you realize that the tribe has accusations lodged against it, step over to the high court and ask that the record book be opened and any recorded accusations be read. Again, if you are familiar with courts of heaven intercession, you may want to have the generational line's records pulled and take care of things in one of the other courts.

But since we are conducting a generational and we are already engaged with the high court, I think it is perfectly acceptable to have accusations resolved there.

For those accusations that are accurate, the blood of Jesus is the answer. If the tribe is guilty of harming itself or others, you cannot plead innocence, but you can plead the finished work of Christ and ask for an acquittal. If the tribe has empowered the enemy by making accusations and wishing harm on others, ask for the blood of Jesus to witness on behalf of the tribe and ask if Jesus is willing to pay any outstanding debts owed by the tribe. Again, an innocent verdict is not possible when a tribe is guilty but, because of Christ, an acquittal is possible. As you ask the court for mercy, keep in mind that the finished work of the Cross is the answer to every opposing argument that may be presented by enemy spirits. Include in your plea that all the negative consequences resulting from accusations be directed away from the tribe to the Cross.

If the accusation is inaccurate, such as the ones in my examples, you can ask for the tribe to be found innocent. Here is a sample prayer for challenging accusations. It is to be presented before the court.

> *As a representative of my bloodline, I repent for myself and my people for making accusations against You, Lord, against Your image, and against Your creation. I repent for believing that we had a right to accuse and condemn. I repent for wishing harm on others. I repent for stepping into the place reserved for Father God (James 4:12). I ask Jesus to empower the words of repentance I have just spoken and for every negative consequence that resulted from our sin be redirected to His Cross.*
>
> *I ask the court to open the books and reveal the accusations that stand against my bloodline. If the accusations are accurate, I ask for forgiveness. Please pay the debts that my people owe to You and to others. Falling on the mercy of the court, I ask for an acquittal to be entered into the books.*

If the accusations are inaccurate, I ask that they be expunged from the books and that an innocent verdict be written in their place.

Please restore whatever has been stolen from my people because of these accusations. Please judge every evil spirit involved in condemning and punishing my tribe.

The work of Christ is a finished work. The blood of Jesus was offered as payment for the sins of all humanity. I call upon His finished work and His blood to witness on behalf of my tribe.

I suggest that you wait before the court to see if there is more that needs to done or if the court wants to bring up another issue. Once you discern that you are released from the court, step back to the timeline and look around. What has changed? If you are free to move forward, continue your restoration by sending the blessing further down the timeline.

Practice

1. Enter the high court. Ask that the records be opened and any trades affecting you personally be revealed. Follow the steps outlined above to have the trades overturned.

2. Stand on your timeline and ask the Holy Spirit to reveal any demonic trades made by your tribe. Investigate any rituals and sacrifices that come to mind. Ask the Lord, "What was traded, and in exchange for what?

3. Ask the high court to open the records and reveal if any accusations exist against your tribe. Practice the sample prayer for challenging accusations, seeking acquittal or innocence.

CHAPTER 16

STRATEGIC PRAYERS AND PROTOCOLS

The prayer of a righteous person is powerful and effective.

James 5:16 NIV

In Chapter 13, I promised to offer some sample strategic prayers and protocols to address any portals, agreements with death, ancestral spirits, and ancestral emotions that you may discover as you restore a generational line. You may want to review Chapter 13.

Unholy Portals

Heinous sin and certain kinds of agreements may tear open the fabric separating the natural world from the fallen supernatural realm occupied by spiritual predators. This creates a portal. If you find an unholy portal as you are cleansing, ask the Lord to show you if it was opened unintentionally as a consequence of sin or of a demonic agreement.

For example, my ministry team and I had approached the Lord asking Him to show us the cause of pathological narcissism. We learned that it begins in the bloodline with a heart belief about identity. A tribe that considers itself completely unacceptable, disgusting, shameful, or worthless is positioned to strike a bargain with any evil being that offers a better identity. Like all demonic trades and agreements, this offer comes at a devastating cost. The tribe's true godly identity is sucked into the background. Remember that the head of the tribe, a leader with followers, and a parent with a family is considered the representative of the entire group. So when the bargain is struck and the tribe's true identity exchanged for one that is allegedly the 'best of the best' — better than all other possible identities — a portal opens and a spirit of pride steps through. This evil being floods the tribe with its own identity, emotions, and thoughts. Now every member of the tribe is subject to this spirit that comes and goes as it pleases.

This is a kind of portal that was opened through deception. Evil spirits are unable to provide a better identity. They can only fake it. Or just be themselves. This is just one kind of unholy portal that might be opened through certain sin or agreements. Notice that the heart belief preceded the tribe's willingness to do whatever it took to exchange its identity.

Other portals are opened intentionally in order to gain some kind of advantage. Remember the two portals that had been opened in Africa? Both were intentionally opened and individuals bound to them.

How to close unintentional unholy portals

Perhaps it is best to begin this process before the high court. Step away from the timeline and approach the bench, offering repentance for what was done. Admit that the sin or agreement was wrong and harmful. Ask the court to allow the sacrifice of Christ to pay the debts owed by the tribe and call for the blood of Christ and His finished work to witness that recompense for these sins has been made.

When closing portals, I ask the court to hold the evil spirits involved in deceiving the tribe accountable for their actions. Then I ask the court to dispatch the angels to close the portal on the timeline, the land, and the atmosphere. If the portal has been established within the tribe or individuals, ask that the angels close those portals and be sent to round up any evil spirits released into the natural realm via the portal and returned to their proper place.

Here are a few more steps to take.

1. Ask that the timeline, land, and atmosphere be healed and restored to its godly function.
2. Ask that the tribe and its people be healed and that all that was stolen be restored.
3. Remain before the court until you are released.

Step back to the timeline and see what has changed. If the portal has closed and there is no more to do, gather up the restoration blessing, send it down the timeline, and continue with your restoration.

Sometimes portals are opened intentionally in order to gain some kind of advantage. Remember the two portals that had been opened in Africa? Both were intentionally opened and individuals bound to them at the time of their opening. It is very likely that the descendants of the tribe that opened the portal have no idea why they are being tormented by the presence of evil spirits. Any agreement made with fallen beings is considered permanent by those beings. This means that descendants are still being bound to an unholy portal by the evil spirits involved in the original agreement.

It is very likely that any portal opened on purpose has a physical location. So be sure to ask the court to have the land deeply healed.

Follow the steps above and add these to them. Always involve the Holy Spirit. Listen to Him because He will refine your appeal so that it fits your situation.

Extra steps for closing intentional unholy portals

1. Repent for partnering with evil to open a portal. Repent for believing the lies that led to this action and for the harm that was done, asking that all debts be paid. Ask Jesus to empower or activate your words of repentance.

2. Ask the court to release the tribe and its members from the portal and from its physical location, including any deceased tribe members who may be bound to the portal. Ask that these ancestors be released and ushered into the presence of the Creator. It is possible the tribe is pinned to that portal's location, so ask that all ties, bonds, and bindings be destroyed and the portal closed.

3. Ask for everything that has been stolen from the tribe and its members be restored.

4. Before you step back to the timeline, ask the court to send healing into any physical location that housed the unholy portal.

Agreements With Death

Tribes that have used death as a way to solve problems are likely to have formed, knowingly or unknowingly, agreements with evil spirits of death. Abortion, infanticide, murder, suicide, and euthanasia are all ways that a tribe can partner with death to solve problems believed to be unsolvable in any other way. This results in spirits of death attaching to the bloodline and tempting the descendants to turn to death whenever they are overwhelmed, resent unwanted responsibilities, or face difficult challenges and problems.

Land and time may be defiled because the tribe participated in rituals involving death or because some kind of violent death happened at the place and at the time.

How to remove ancestral agreements with death

This may be done in the high court whenever you discover an ancestral agreement with death on the timeline. Step from the timeline to the high court.

Begin with repentance for turning to death as an answer instead of turning to the Lord. The reason for not turning to the Lord will vary from tribe to tribe. Find out the reason (the heart belief) and repent. Use this prayer as a model.

> *Lord, on behalf of myself and my people I repent for using death as a way to solve difficult problems, escape unwanted responsibilities, and avoid pain. I ask Jesus to empower my words of repentance. Please also forgive us for not running to You, the giver of life. Because of our sin we have incurred debts that we cannot pay. Please pay our debts, making right what we have made wrong.*
>
> *In Jesus name. Amen.*

If you are shown that the tribe wished death on others or cursed others with death, add that to your repentance prayer and also ask that all evil wishes and curses be destroyed at the Cross.

Here is a short list of other considerations to bring before the court.

1. Ask that the reaping for these sins be directed away from the tribe and toward the Cross.
2. Ask that any defiled land and any defiled time be cleansed and healed.
3. Repudiate all benefits gained by making agreements with death.
4. Ask the court to annul the tribe's agreements with death.
5. Ask that any blessings gained whenever the tribe chose life or when it did turn to the Lord be released to the descendants.

Wait on the court until you know that you are released, then step back to the timeline and see if anything has changed. If the agreement has been removed, gather up the restoration blessing and send it further along the timeline.

> *The thief comes only to steal and kill and destroy; I have come that they may have life, and have it to the full.*
>
> John 10:10

Ancestral Spirits and How to Remove Them

It is best to avoid speaking to demons or any other fallen celestial being. But a human spirit may be spoken to. If you discern that a human spirit, or spirits, is clinging to the bloodline, step into the high court and ask that these spirits be brought before the Judge. Now, you may run into resistance if the human spirits are afraid, or if they have been captured by the demonic.

If these human spirits are afraid to go into the Lord's presence, ask who is in charge and open a discussion with that person. You will be using your spiritual discernment to hear and/or see this human spirit. Begin by asking why the spirit remained on earth. The reasons usually are as follows. The spirit is confused and does not know that returning to the Creator is an option. The spirit is afraid of God. The spirit wants to remain on the earth to look after a loved one or after beloved land. The spirit is bound to land, time, or to a portal. I once spoke with a human spirit that refused to go to the Lord upon death because he had been told that there are no dogs in heaven. He loved his dog and did not want to go to a heaven without his dog. The Lord showed this person that his dog was already in heaven waiting for him. The spirit then willingly went into the presence of God. The other main reason that spirits are afraid is because they have either been captured by enemy angelic spirits or dedicated to them.

If the spirit is unable to communicate, it most likely has an evil spirit guard. In such cases it is usually possible for the captive human spirit to nod or shake its head. Ask if it has been taken captive or if it is being guarded. If it nods, say this: *I ask Jesus through the power of His blood to break the assignment of the demon assigned to this person. I ask the Lord to rebuke it and to reassign it to the feet of Jesus. Angels, take it there now.*

In my experience, this removes the demonic guard, making it possible for the human spirit to communicate.

When I discover the presence of ancestral human spirits, I open a conversation by asking why they did not return to the Creator at the time of death. Once I have a grasp on the reasons, I ask the Holy Spirit how to make it safe for this human and any others with it to go into the presence of Creator God. I then follow the Holy Spirit's instructions, continuing to interact until the human spirits are willing to be escorted by either Jesus or His holy angels into God's presence.

Once these spirits are removed, I ask the court to release cleansing to the bloodline that removes any emotions, structures, and detritus left behind by these spirits. If there is any repentance or forgiveness that needs to be accomplished because of the tribe's heart beliefs and decisions that led to their dead being unable or unwilling to go to God, address that in the high court.

Ancestral Emotions

Unresolved emotion is going to go somewhere. Unresolved generational emotion is transferred to the children who then transfer it to their children and so on. This means that the current living tribe members carry emotion that is not theirs. It is impossible to process another person's emotions, so this causes confusion and may be the cause of some depressions, anxieties, and even mental illnesses.

How to remove downloaded generational emotions

A simple prayer has been my approach to this problem. I rarely present this prayer before a heavenly court. You can do that, of course. I just have not found it to be necessary. Here is how I pray. Please modify the prayer as the Lord leads you.

Lord God, please forgive me and my people for failing to correctly process our emotions. Forgive us for downloading them into our children and teaching our children to do the same to theirs. Please cleanse the bloodline of all unprocessed emotions and remove them. Cleanse all the living descendants of these ancestral emotions. Separate my emotions from the emotions of others, so that I only feel what is mine to feel.

Cleanse me of all the confusion, depression, anxiety, and/or mental illness that is the result of feeling someone else's emotions and trying to process someone else's emotions.

Teach me how to process my emotions correctly, so that I do not continue the habit of downloading them into the next generation. If I am unable to process the emotions that I am feeling, remind me to sit with You until I am able to manage my emotions in a healthy way that brings honor to You.

Each of these prayers and strategies are meant to serve as models. When before the court and before the Lord always lean into exactly what you need to pray and do in order to resolve the issue on the bloodline. Keep in mind that this process is very organic and may become messy. Perseverance is your friend. Just recently, my ministry team and I were conducting a generational cleanse when we saw a courtroom turned on its side. It was several minutes before we realized that the tribe had overturned justice. We had been praying about something completely different and this image helped direct our attention where it really needed to be.

Let us not become weary in doing good, for at the proper time we will reap a harvest if we do not give up.

Galatians 6:9 NIV

Practice

1. As you are cleansing your timeline, ask the Holy Spirit to reveal any unholy portals. If found, practice the high court protocol for closing any unintentional portals, noting changes on the timeline.

2. Imagine presenting the prayer for an intentional portal in the high court, including repentance for partnering with evil and asking for healing of the physical location. Reflect on how the land's healing might manifest.

3. If you suspect an agreement with death (e.g., family patterns of suicide or abortion), rehearse the high court prayer, focusing on repenting for the heart belief and redirecting curses to the cross.

4. Pray the ancestral emotions prayer aloud, asking God to "Separate my emotions from the emotions of others, so that I only feel what is mine to feel." Journal any shifts in emotions or clarity afterward.

CHAPTER 17

JUSTICE IS SERVED

How the oppressor has ceased, and how the onslaught has ceased!
The Lord has broken the staff of the wicked, the scepter of rulers, which used to strike the peoples in fury with unceasing strokes, which subdued the nations in anger with unrestrained persecution.
The whole earth is at rest and is quiet; they break forth into shouts of joy.

Isaiah 14:4-7

IT IS MY PRAYER THAT this book has helped you understand the importance of the tribal heart — the central belief shaping your family's perception of reality. I pray that you have learned how to locate the foundational heart belief that is driving the behaviors and attitudes of your tribe and have learned how to help others do the same. As you walk with the Lord through the repentance and restoration process, many blessings will emerge. These blessings are yours and also belong to those you love and to those yet to be born.

After extending your restoration blessing to all your living relatives and sending it down the generational line, return to the high court. There is one more step left. But before we take it, I want to tell you a story in the hopes of encouraging you to pursue cleansing your generational line. This happened when I was just being introduced to generational healing. The Lord had begun to draw my attention to a dark feeling of doom that was hanging over me. I called Tom Hawkins to ask his opinion and he suggested that the feeling was a generational issue. His observation started me on this journey. As I worked to cleanse my generational line, I discovered that a deep fear of the Lord was hidden within the heart of my maternal tribe. That fear was producing the feeling of inescapable doom coming down from above. Addressing the tribal heart belief that God wanted to hurt us and following the steps I have outlined in this book lifted the sense of being doomed from above and made it possible to connect more comfortably with God. This experience showed me the power of addressing generational issues, which leads us to the final step in the heavenly court. Be assured that it is a safe step. For those who are unfamiliar with spiritual warfare, know that God's grace protects you as you engage in this process.

Do you recall the evil spirits being held in the holding area? These beings are on trial for attacking your bloodline with the intention of either twisting or eradicating the expression of God that He has placed there. They have lodged a claim against you and your people because of ancient agreements, trades, and sins. They are claiming a legal right to bind all the people because each subsequent generation has either agreed with or been complicit with these ancient iniquities. But you have taken a stand on behalf of your people and you have repented, repudiating all benefits gained through any kind of commerce with the demonic. You have asked the court to cancel all agreements and overturn all trades. You have asked for forgiveness and declared that the blood of Jesus and His finished work is enough to pay all debts. Now it is time to ask for justice. Keep in mind that the spirits are restrained by God. They cannot hurt you. You are His child, wrapped in His grace and favor.

Ask the court to judge the fallen entities being held in the holding area. Here is a sample petition.

> *I petition the heavenly court on behalf of my bloodline, asking that every evil spirit harming my tribe be judged for their crimes against God's creation and image. May they be rebuked to the fullest extent allowed — honor for honor, dishonor for dishonor — and forbidden to retaliate as well as restrained from further attacks.*
>
> *May all stolen blessings be restored in Jesus' name.*

Then I like to stand before the high court and watch God's justice shine.

As you stand there in the courts of heaven, watching the tormentors of your people being carried away, what might be the result of your restoration work? What glorious blessings might your family line release into the earth?

Practice

1. Write a personal version of the petition provided in the chapter, tailoring it to your tribe. Speak it aloud in a quiet space, visualizing yourself standing in the high court. Reflect on how it feels to ask for justice and restoration.

2. Read Isaiah 14:4–7 slowly, focusing on the phrases *"the whole earth is at rest"* and *"shouts of joy."* Journal about what *"rest"* and *"joy"* might look like for your tribe after the restoration process.

3. What emotions or thoughts arise when you imagine standing in the high court to petition for justice for your bloodline? How can you lean on faith to overcome any hesitation?

APPENDIX

Thanks to the late Dr. Tom Hawkins, founder of *Restoration In Christ Ministries*, for providing a model for heavenly appeals.

An Example of a Heavenly Appeal for an Individual

The following appeal was written for a little girl who was being tormented. The parents had tried all they knew to stop the torment. They asked me to write and help them offer an appeal. It did succeed in stopping the torment.

This sample is drawn from an actual appeal written for a female child. Please change the wording and the pronouns as needed. Heavenly appeals should be designed with the individual in mind.

Opening petition to be presented in the high court

In the name and authority of the true Yeshua, Jesus Christ the Messiah, the One who was born of the virgin Mary, having lived from all eternity, being one with the Father, and who having died on the Cross was raised from the dead and is even now seated at the right hand of the Father, we bring this request before the One who sits on the throne, Yahweh the Supreme God, the One True God, the Only God, the Lord of the Hosts of Heaven, the One who is the Eternal, Sovereign Creator of the universe, the One who is Holy, Just and Righteous.

In accordance with Isaiah 33:22, which states,

> *The Lord is our judge, the Lord is our lawgiver, the Lord is our king; it is He who will save us.*

We ask for You to sit as judge and render judgment against the evil forces that have attacked one of Your own.

We petition You, the Most High God, who is the only judge and lawgiver, according to James 4:12, that You allow us to present a court case on behalf of the one known as _____, born on _____(date).

_____ has been attacked, abused and tormented by spirits that refuse to bow the knee to the name of Your Holy Son when spoken on her behalf by her parents and other believers. These beings have defied the authority given to us by Your Son, Jesus Christ in Matthew 10:8 when He commanded us to cast out demons. They have refused to return to _____ her freedom, her mind, or her confidence in her relationship with You. We believe that this is not acceptable.

Because of that torment, _____ is unable to represent herself, so her father and her mother are here to represent their daughter.

Recognition of the Son as Advocate

Most High God, we submit before the court that Jesus Christ Himself is the Chief Cornerstone. He is our heavenly lawyer and so we petition that whatever we argue that is not in accordance with Your word and with truth, or however poorly we might argue, that our Head Lawyer, our true Advocate, Jesus Christ of Nazareth, be allowed to make all necessary corrections to any of our errors, mistakes and misunderstandings, through the intercessory ministry of the Holy Spirit of the living God, and to make these things right before You.

We further petition the court that _____'s parents be allowed to speak on behalf of the plaintiff.

We further submit, Most High God, that the eyes of _____'s heart might be enlightened so that she might know the hope to which You have called her and the riches of Your glorious inheritance in the saints and Your incomparably great power for her because she believes. Lord, that power is like the working of Your mighty strength which You exerted in Christ when You raised Him from the dead and seated Him at Your right hand in the heavenly realms far above all rule and authority, power and dominion, every title that can be given in the present age but also in the age to come.

Now, Most High God, we submit before the court that You have placed all things under the feet of our Savior Jesus, and appointed Him to be the Head over everything for the Church, which is Your Body, the fullness of You who fills everything in every way (from Ephesians 1:18–23).

The Charge

Most High God we are fully aware that the defense will claim that _____ has been guilty of various sins and crimes which the defense will present as evidence against her. They will also bring charges against her based upon the sins of her ancestors.

But we bring evidence before the court that _____ is Your blood-bought daughter, having accepted Jesus Christ as Savior when she was _____ (age) on _____ (date) before witnesses. She was water baptized in the name of Your Son on _____ date before witnesses. She has been heard to profess Jesus Christ as the Son of God and her Savior by witnesses.

We report before You, God, that she is guilty of being a sinner by birth and by choice and, like us all, has fallen short of Your glory. Even now, when tormented by evil spirits, she cries out her sins and failings, she mourns over her mistakes.

But we submit to the Court that whatever she has done intentionally or whatever was forced upon her is covered by the blood of her Savior, the true Jesus Christ of Nazareth, the King of kings and the Lord of lords. She admits to the sins of her forefathers as well as her own guilt. Insofar as is possible, she has sought to acknowledge her sin and we would claim that sin covered by the atonement of our Lord Jesus Christ whose payment has fully satisfied Your righteous requirements.

That evil spirits would torment her and refuse to obey the commands of Your children to release her is an insult to the finished work of Christ. In essence by refusing to release her they are proclaiming that the work of Your Son on her behalf is not enough or finished. That is not acceptable.

Thus, we ask You to charge all involved evil spirits and entities, including malicious human spirits that are without repentance, with the crime of seeking to invalidate the work of Christ in _____'s life as well as to belittle Him and His finished work in the lives of her family. We call upon You, Judge of all that lives, to render vengeance upon them, based on Jeremiah 11:20.

> *Lord of armies, who judges righteously,*
> *Who puts the feelings and the heart to the test,*
> *Let me see Your vengeance on them,*
> *For to You I have committed my cause.*

Repentance By Parents

Parents now confess Jesus Christ as Lord and Savior before the court.

They then repent for all generational involvement in witchcraft and blood magic; for all covenants made with evil entities, and especially for resourcing the children, using them as commodities, stealing their life force, identity, purpose and future.

Just a simple repentance is needed. The parents take turns.

They admit to being the descendants of the people who committed such crimes. They ask for forgiveness and restoration, and that the court extend the mercy of the Cross to them and to their people, based on Lamentations 3:22–23, which promises:

> *The Lord's acts of mercy indeed do not end. For His compassions do not fail. They are new every morning; Great is Your faithfulness.*

Leader:

In light of the parents' repentance I am asking that the web of fear woven over and into the tribes be dissolved. For as it is written in Psalm 103:10–13, You are a God of compassion.

> *He has not dealt with us according to our sins,*
> *Nor rewarded us according to our guilty deeds.*

> *For as high as the heavens are above the earth,*
> *So great is His mercy toward those who fear Him.*
> *As far as the east is from the west,*
> *So far has He removed our wrongdoings from us.*
> *Just as a father has compassion on his children,*
> *So the Lord has compassion on those who fear Him.*

Lord, we contend that this web of fear woven and held together by ancestral sin and the evil entities of fear, intimidation, and control is not everlasting.

Rather, as Psalm 103:17 says:

> *Your Mercy is from everlasting to everlasting for those who fear You,*
> *And Your justice belongs to the children's children.*

So we are asking that the wind of Your Holy Spirit pass over this web of fear so that it is no more and its place no longer remembers it.

Present the Promises of God

Parents present God's word concerning their child before the court. (Whatever Scripture the Lord has directed the parents to include. Simply state His word).

Closing

> As the Israelites cried out to You for justice in Psalm 83:1–3 & 13–18, we come before You asking for justice for _____ and her family.

> *God, do not remain quiet;*
> *Do not be silent and, God, do not be still.*
> *For behold, Your enemies make an uproar, And those who hate You have exalted themselves.*

They make shrewd plans against Your people,
And conspire together against Your treasured ones.

My God, make them like the whirling dust,
Like chaff before the wind.
Like fire that burns the forest,
And like a flame that sets the mountains on fire,
So pursue them with Your heavy gale,
And terrify them with Your storm.
Fill their faces with dishonor,
*So that they will seek Your Name, L*ORD*.*
May they ever be ashamed and dismayed forever,
And may they be humiliated and perish,
*So that they will know that You alone, whose name is the L*ORD*,*
are the Most High over all the earth.

We petition the court of the Most High God, that You render a judgment on behalf of Your covenant child _____, who is covered by the blood of the eternal covenant and made secure by the death of Your Son, the Lord Jesus Christ.

We ask that You render judgment against all involved evil cosmic beings and entities; all demons and the humans who participated in her abuse. We ask that they not be allowed to transfer assignments, receive any other help, and that all the levels under them be brought into judgment as well.

According to Ephesians 1, _____ is Your chosen adopted child, holy and blameless in Your sight, whom You have marked with a seal, the promised Holy Spirit.

She has been blessed with every spiritual blessing in the heavenlies but instead of enjoying those blessings is experiencing horrible abuse and silence in the heavens. This is not in accordance with Your will or Word and, thus, is not acceptable.

We have argued our case as we understand it, in accordance with our limited understanding of the absolute truth of Your Word, but we plead the intercessory ministry of Your Holy Spirit who intercedes for us with groans that words cannot express. We take comfort in the truth that He who searches our hearts knows the mind of the Spirit, because the Spirit intercedes for the saints in accordance with Your will (from Romans 8:26–27).

We further ask the court that however we have failed to argue correctly or have misunderstood Your Word and Your will, that our Heavenly Lawyer, the Lord Jesus Christ make whatever corrections are necessary before the court and that His corrections be entered into the record. Most High God, Lord of all the Hosts of Heaven, we ask You to render judgment on behalf of Your covenant child, _____, and give her redress of grievances we have brought before the court.

We ask You to render Your judgment against the beings now being held in Your court and that You allow us further opportunity to bring additional information from time to time as we become aware of it. We plead all of the above in the matchless name and authority of our Lord and Savior Jesus Christ of Nazareth, the King of kings and Lord of lords. Amen

You caused judgment to be heard from heaven;
The earth feared and was still
When God arose to judgment,
To save all the humble of the earth.

Psalm 76:8–9

Follow this formal appeal by asking the participants if they want to add anything or if they discerned anything.

Wait upon the Lord until everyone feels released.

WORKS CITED

Bowman, Susan. *The Performing Heart: How to Escape the Trap of Relentless Performing and Enter the Security of God's Rest.* North Hampton, NH: Mindstir Media, 2023.

Burk, Arthur. *Relentless Generational Blessings.* Whittier, CA: Plumbline Ministries, 2003.

McCraty, Rollin. *Science of the Heart: Exploring the Role of the Heart in Human Performance.* Vol. 2. Boulder Creek, CA: HeartMath Institute, 2015.

McCraty, Rollin, Mike Atkinson, and Dana Tomasino. *Science of the Heart: Exploring the Role of the Heart in Human Performance.* Publication no. 01-001. Boulder Creek, CA: HeartMath Institute, 2001.

Nam, Jane. "First-Generation College Student Facts." BestColleges, April 12, 2023. https://www.bestcolleges.com/research/first-generation-students-facts-statistics/.

Sandford, John L. and R. Loren Sandford. *The Renewal of the Mind.* Tulsa: Victory House, Inc., 1991.

Strong, James. *Strong's Expanded Exhaustive Concordance of the Bible.* Nashville: Thomas Nelson, 2009.

STUDY GUIDE
AND
SMALL GROUP DISCUSSION QUESTIONS

Chapter 1: We All Begin Somewhere

Questions:

1. Reflect on the circumstances of your family during your childhood. Consider financial status, cultural background, and major events. How might these have shaped your sense of identity or expectations about life? Can you identify one belief you hold that might stem from these circumstances?

2. What strengths or gifts do you see in your family? Is your family generous, hospitable, creative, loyal, persistent? How might these reflect God's design for your tribe?

3. What is the tribal heart belief system and how does it differ from personal beliefs?

4. Distinguish between the blessing of righteousness and the blessing of design. Why is the design blessing more significant for your bloodline's restoration? (Romans 11:29)

5. Why does a tribe bury the memory of traumatic events?

6. Why is spiritual discernment so important when restoring a generational line?

Small Group Discussion Questions

1. Luke 6:45 describes the heart as a storehouse. Why do you think the belief system stored within the heart is so resistant to change? What might make accessing this "storehouse" both challenging and rewarding?

2. Discerned spiritual realities are often meant to be understood as symbolic rather than literal. Why might believers, even mature ones, struggle to interpret spiritual experiences symbolically? How could this misunderstanding affect their approach to generational restoration? Discuss a time you misinterpreted a spiritual experience.

3. How does John 16:13's promise of the Holy Spirit's guidance build confidence in uncovering hidden tribal beliefs? Share an example of a family pattern that might stem from a buried trauma.

Chapter 2: Is That You, God, or Just My Imagination?

Questions:

1. What are the three key beliefs hidden in the tribal heart, and how might they shape your family's interactions with the world?

2. Why does God choose to communicate through senses like seeing, hearing, or feeling rather than direct, literal messages? How does this approach deepen our reliance on the Holy Spirit? Why is practicing discernment through the senses essential for restoration?

3. Why are vague impressions or fleeting sounds easy to dismiss, and how can journaling help you discern their meaning?

4. How does the inward witness (warm fuzzy vs. cold yukky) guide interpretation of spiritual realities, and why should you trust it over intellectual reasoning? If an interpretation doses not "feel" right to you, what should you do?

5. Of the five senses, which one is Satan most likely to use in an effort to deceive you? What is a way that you can protect yourself from being deceived by what you hear?

6. How do emotions like shame or despair during restoration reveal tribal heart beliefs, and why should you avoid assuming they are yours?

Small Group Discussion Questions

1. How does God's use of familiar imagery (e.g., an elephant meaning football or strength) reflect His intimate knowledge of you? Share a personal example of a vision or impression and its interpretation.

2. Why might Christians distrust their imagination as a God-given tool for discernment? Discuss how reframing it as a gift could enhance your spiritual growth.

Chapter 3: When An Elephant Is Not An Elephant

Questions:

1. Why is accurate interpretation of spiritual realities challenging, and how can relying on the Holy Spirit prevent jumping to conclusions?

2. How might cultural differences in your family or community shape the symbols God uses to speak to you? Why is it important to consider your personal and cultural lens when interpreting spiritual experiences?

3. Are the spiritual realities you experience meant to be understood literally? How are they supposed to be understood most of the time? Are there exceptions to this rule?

4. Compare the symbolic dreams of Pharaoh (Genesis 41) with the literal dreams of Joseph (Matthew 2:13). Why might God use different approaches for different people?

Small Group Discussion Questions

1. How do biblical metaphors like Jesus as the "good shepherd" deepen your understanding of God's nature? Share a metaphor from scripture or life that resonates with you.

2. How did the "pink doll" vision reflect the little girl's heart belief, and what does this teach about interpreting symbolic visions?

3. Why might God tailor spiritual imagery to your experiences, and how does this encourage trust in His communication during restoration? Discuss a symbol from a dream or vision and its personal meaning.

Chapter 4: The Heart Is A Boss

Questions:

1. How does neurocardiology support the biblical view of the physical heart as a thinking and feeling organ?
2. How does the tribal heart belief system influence personal beliefs, and why is it resistant to change?
3. Why are most heart beliefs painful, and how do children use inner vows to manage this pain?
4. What is more critical for restoration: historical events or the beliefs formed from them? Why?
5. How does the heart's role as a belief storehouse explain persistent generational patterns?

Small Group Discussion Questions

1. How does Proverbs 4:23's emphasis on guarding the heart reshape your view of its role in spiritual life? Discuss a time a heart belief influenced your decisions.
2. Why might hidden vows perpetuate harmful patterns across generations? Share how identifying a vow could lead to freedom in your family.

Chapter 5: You Are What Your Heart Believes

Questions:

1. How does the heart build beliefs from early experiences, and why can't changing your thoughts alone shift these beliefs?
2. How might a tribal belief like "we are always victims" explain recurring family patterns, and how can identifying it bring clarity?
3. Why does the heart's use of absolute language (e.g., "always," "never") lock in tribal beliefs, and how does this differ from the mind's flexibility?
4. Why is focusing on heart beliefs more effective than traditional models that address sin and trauma? (John Sandford's principle)
5. How does Freemasonry exploit tribal beliefs about powerlessness, and what promises does it make to address these?

Small Group Discussion Questions

1. Dr. Armour's research highlights the heart's ability to learn, remember, and sense independently. How does this scientific understanding reshape your view of biblical references to the heart, such as Proverbs 4:23? What might it mean to "guard your heart" in light of this?
2. Tribal heart beliefs amplify personal ones, such as always feeling unfairly treated. How might identifying a tribal belief help you understand recurring patterns in your family? Can you think of a specific example where a tribal belief has influenced your perception of an event?
3. The heart speaks in absolutes using words such as always and never. Why do you think the heart is so rigid in its beliefs compared to the mind's flexibility? How might this rigidity manifest in your relationships or decision-making?

Chapter 6: Starting Point

Questions:

1. The seminar described at the beginning of Chapter 6 dissolved into chaos. Why do you think that happened and how does a structured approach prevent this?
2. Why is starting at the Tower of Babel more effective than recent family history for uncovering root beliefs?
3. What two cataclysmic traumas shape every tribe's heart, and how might blaming God for them affect how He is viewed?

Small Group Discussion Questions

1. The seminar dissolved into chaos due to lack of structure and differing opinions. Why do you think a lack of structure can derail a generational cleanse? How might a structured approach, like the one proposed, build confidence in the process?
2. Beliefs, not historical events, are the root of generational issues. Why is focusing on beliefs more effective than tracing specific times or places? How does this shift your approach to restoration?
3. Starting at the Tower of Babel ensures the cleanse begins before significant tribal beliefs solidified. Why is this more effective than starting with more recent history?
4. Tribes carry within their hearts trauma from the Flood and Babel, often blaming God for these events. How might misdirected blame shape a tribe's beliefs about God, others, or life? Can you think of modern examples where trauma leads to blaming the wrong person or thing?

Chapter 7: Mercy, Grace, And Weirdness Abound

Questions:

1. What is the purpose of the opening prayer? Which spiritual beings does it address? How do you feel about speaking to angels or demons?
2. How does God use imagery that is familiar to you?
3. What is a heavenly appeal? What is its purpose? How does it differ from a generational restoration?
4. Why is it possible for a visit to the throne room to be unpleasant? What emotions may surface? How should you interpret them?
5. What are inner vows and how do they lock heart beliefs into place?

Small Group Discussion Questions

1. Hebrews 4:16 describes the throne room as a place of mercy and grace. Why is this an ideal starting point for generational restoration, especially given the potential hostility of tribal beliefs toward God?
2. The beginning prayer asserts authority over evil spirits and invites angelic protection. Why is it important to establish these boundaries before entering the spiritual realm? How does praying "in the name of Jesus" ground this authority biblically?
3. Inner vows lock heart beliefs in place and attract evil spirits. How do these vows and spirits perpetuate generational patterns? Why is breaking vows and reassigning spirits a critical step in clearing blockages?

Chapter 8: All Rise; Court is in Session

Questions:

1. What should you do if you are not given permission to go to the high court? Why might this happen?
2. How might you experience (see) the high court? Why does that experience differ from culture to culture and person to person?
3. Who sits as judge in the high court?
4. What claims do evil spirits make against your tribe? Why is it common for tribes to agree that they deserve to be punished?
5. How do you prove that you have standing in the court, and why is claiming Christ's redemption essential?
6. Why is it best to work with one side of the bloodline at a time?
7. List the blocking vows. How can you discern that blocking vows are activated? How do you break them? What do you need to send away after you have broken them?

Small Group Discussion Questions

1. You must establish your standing as a biological or adopted descendant of the bloodline in order to represent it. You must also establish that you are a child of God before proceeding with a generational. Why is it essential to accept your tribal identity, even if painful, in order to represent your bloodline? How does claiming Christ's redemption strengthen your position in the court?
2. Blocking vows are made to avoid the pain of what is believed. How do these vows distort a tribe's perception of reality? Why is breaking them critical for accessing the blessings needed for restoration?

Chapter 9: The Framework

Questions:

1. You are searching to discover what the tribe believes about three areas: What are those areas?
2. Why is finding the first significant trauma important? What is built around that first significant trauma?
3. What are the signs to watch for as you roll your restoration blessings down the first 500 years? What do those signs indicate?
4. What questions should you ask the Holy Spirit when the restoration blessings are stopped by one of the symbols indicating a trauma or a problem that needs to be investigated?

Small Group Discussion Questions

1. Chapter 9 compares a generational restoration without structure to confusing physical therapy exercises. Why does a structured framework help limit confusion and maintain focus on tribal heart beliefs? How might chaos derail the process, as seen in the Chapter 6 seminar?
2. Traumas like famine, plague, or loss shape tribal beliefs. Why do these events lead to painful heart beliefs? How might the tribe's initial fear of God, post-Babel, amplify these beliefs?
3. Traumas similar to the original event repeat due to the tribe's belief that "life will always go badly for us in a specific way." How does a belief hidden in the heart shape a tribe's perception of its circumstances?

Chapter 10: The Timeline

Questions:

1. What do bumps, roadblocks, ditches, and pits reveal? What should you do when you encounter them?
2. When you come to a barrier, what questions should you ask? What is the most important question?
3. What do paths, roads, and landscapes reveal? Why do you think these often start out well but become desolate? What does this shift suggest?
4. What are some of the emotions you might feel as you explore your generational timeline? What are these emotions meant to reveal? What should you avoid doing when you feel strong emotion during a generational restoration?
5. What is the easiest way to recognize heart beliefs? What kind of language does the heart use? What kind of emotion usually accompanies a heart belief? What are some examples of emphatic statements that reveal what the heart believes?

Small Group Discussion Questions

1. Chapter 10 emphasizes sticking to the Chapter 9 structure to avoid getting lost in spiritual experiences. Why is maintaining this focus on tribal heart beliefs critical for a successful restoration? How might fascination with spiritual realities (e.g., vivid visions) derail the process?
2. Bumps, roadblocks, ditches, and pits signal significant traumas or decisions. Why do these barriers manifest symbolically, and how do they help pinpoint the formation of tribal heart beliefs? How does this align with the symbolic language discussed in Chapters 2–3?

3. Minor traumas can spark significant and painful beliefs if they hit a tribe's core. How might a tribe's unique gifting make it vulnerable to specific traumas? Why is this insight key to restoration?

Chapter 11: Alligators and Carousels: Dismantling Tribal Heart Beliefs

Questions:

1. What is a completed belief? What kinds of questions does a completed belief answer?
2. How do vows to *never forget* affect a heart belief? Why are vows made to *do whatever it takes?* What is that vow trying to manage?
3. Describe the dismantling process. Why is it necessary to repeatedly instruct the heart?
4. Why do you need to break vows? How does that help the heart?
5. What severs a tribe from its identity, and why is restoring it key to a restoration?

Small Group Discussion Questions

1. Chapter 11 emphasizes a methodical approach to dismantling heart beliefs in order to help manage confusion and emotions. Why is structure particularly important when dealing with the "murky unprocessed tribal emotions" that surface? How might those confusing emotions derail a generational restoration?
2. Vows lock beliefs in place and attract evil spirits. How do these vows and the presence of evil spirits reinforce tribal patterns? Why is breaking vows and removing spirits essential before instructing the heart?

Chapter 12: Reconciliation

Questions:

1. Why would the Lord ask you to revisit the tribe's first wrong belief? How many times do you think you should revisit that foundational heart belief?

2. What flows from the tribe's foundational heart belief? Why is resolving the foundational lie-based heart belief the most important thing to do?

3. How are lesser heart beliefs formed? What are they linked to? How are lesser heart beliefs dismantled? Why do you think it is sometimes easier to find lesser heart beliefs?

4. Why is it necessary to accept that you are a member of your tribe? How might accepting your tribe, as an act of obedience to God, open the door to discovering its hidden glory?

5. What happens when a tribe has unpaid debts? Why is it pointless to attempt to pay these kinds of debts yourself? What is the one way those debts can be paid?

Small Group Discussion Questions

1. The foundational heart belief is the fountainhead for all subsequent beliefs and sins. Why is dismantling this belief critical for sustainable freedom? How does it influence lesser beliefs and tribal behaviors?

2. The heart's all-or-nothing way of believing distorts reality. Why does the heart amplify a single event into a universal truth? How does this contribute to a tribe's damaged identity?

3. Why is personal repentance necessary, even for beliefs formed by ancestors? How does this act of repentance at the Cross help to restore the tribe's God-given identity?

4. Unpaid tribal debts lead to guilt, shame, and regret. Why can't the tribe pay these debts itself, and how does Christ's sacrifice address this burden? How does accepting His payment honor Him and enable healing?

Chapter 13: Wonders, Terrors, and Treasures

Questions:

1. What is the symbolic meaning implied by the wheels in Ezekiel's vision? How would knowing the symbolic meaning be useful to Ezekiel? Would knowing the literal meaning have been helpful to him? Why or why not?
2. When you begin the restoration, you are looking for the foundational heart belief. What should you do if you do not find the foundational heart belief? What will help you identify it?
3. How should big sins be handled? Why is resolving the heart beliefs the first step?
4. How are unholy portals discerned? How may an unholy portal prevent effective deliverance?
5. What defiles land or time? How may a tribe become stuck to land or time?
6. How might a demonic agreement made by ancestors affect you?

Small Group Discussion Questions

1. Opening unholy portals begin with a tribe's heart belief. Why is addressing the underlying heart belief important when closing the portal?
2. How do trauma bonds to land, time, persons, or objects perpetuate tribal pain across generations? Why is releasing the tribe through repentance and cleansing the heart belief essential for restoration?
3. The deaf and dumb spirit, the spirit of unbelief, and the spirit of control work together to hide truth and maintain tribal secrets. In what ways do these spirits affect how reality is perceived?
4. Tribal gifts are targeted by the enemy but never removed by God. How does uncovering these gifts restore a tribe's purpose?

Chapter 14: The Blame Game

Questions:

1. Why are humans prone to blame the wrong thing? What subgroups inside a tribe might be singled out and blamed? Reflect on your family dynamics. Is there a subgroup (the men, the women, the children, the father, the mother) that is often assigned blame for any problems? How might this reflect a tribal heart belief?

2. What good things and perfect gifts might a tribe blame for its trauma and pain?

3. What are the two kinds of judgments? Explain how they are different. What is the problem with 'krino' judgment?

4. Why does the victim tribe develop behaviors that mirror the tribe it judged?

Small Group Discussion Questions

1. Tribes tend to blame subgroups within the tribe to justify abuse or neglect. Why does blaming a subgroup create a fertile ground for spirits of abuse?

2. God-given qualities such as innocence, trust, and joy may be blamed for traumas. Why does blaming these qualities equate to blaming God Himself?

3. Chapter 14 distinguishes between condemning ('krino') and discerning ('anakrino') judgment. Why is 'krino' judgment particularly damaging in a generational context? How can practicing 'anakrino' judgment help uncover heart beliefs without reaping condemnation?

4. Because of the law of sowing and reaping, victim tribes that 'krino' judge their oppressors will repeat the behaviors that they condemn. How does repentance for condemning judgments break this cycle?

5. Judging any part of creation, including fallen beings, is judging the Creator. Why does this lead to reaping judgment, and how does it tie to the tribe's underlying anger at God? How can repentance bring this cycle to an end?

Chapter 15: Trades and Accusations

Questions:

1. What was the action that filled Satan with sin and violence, according to Ezekiel 28:16? Why is Satan and other fallen celestial beings eager to trade with humanity? What do they gain and who do they gain access to?

2. How may one person's trading bind an entire tribe or group? Why is the high court the place to overturn it?

3. How do accusations empower evil spirits to attack a tribe? Why is it important to challenge accusations in the high court rather than in the court of hell?

4. How does the blood of Jesus address accurate versus inaccurate accusations?

Small Group Discussion Questions

1. Demonic trades come with a 'forever' tag. What does this mean? Why are these trades so deceptive, and how do they exploit a tribe's vulnerabilities or ambitions?

2. Why can a leader's trade bind an entire tribe or group spiritually? How does this reflect the principle of representation in the spiritual realm?

3. Accusations, even if untrue, empower attacks. Why do accusations provide grounds for demonic attack, and how does challenging them in the high court neutralize them?

4. The blood of Jesus is the answer to both accurate and inaccurate accusations. Why is the finished work of the Cross sufficient to overturn trades and acquit tribes, regardless of guilt? How does this reflect God's mercy?

Chapter 16: Strategic Prayers and Protocols

Questions:

1. What additional steps are needed to close intentional portals compared to unintentional ones?
2. How do agreements with death form, and what are the consequences for descendants? Why is it important to cleanse defiled land or time when addressing death agreements?
3. Why might the dead refuse to go to God, and how are the ancestral dead removed?
4. What are ancestral emotions, and how do they affect living tribe members?

Small Group Discussion Questions

1. Heart beliefs can lead to demonic trades that open unholy portals. Why is cleansing these beliefs critical before closing a portal?
2. Chapter 16 distinguishes between portals opened through deception (unintentional) and those opened deliberately (intentional). Why do intentional portals require additional steps, such as healing the physical location? How does this reflect the deeper spiritual entanglement?
3. Agreements with death stem from beliefs that death solves unsolvable problems. Why do these agreements empower spirits of death across generations, and how does repenting for the underlying heart belief break their hold?
4. Unprocessed ancestral emotions may cause confusion or mental health issues. Why can't descendants process these emotions, and how does separating "me from not me" restore clarity and emotional health?

5. The sideways courtroom example highlights the organic, sometimes messy nature of restoration. Why is perseverance, as emphasized in Galatians 6:9, essential when unexpected spiritual realities arise? How does the guidance of the Holy Spirit ensure adaptability in these messy moments?

Chapter 17: Justice is Served

Questions:

1. How has the process of identifying and repenting for generational iniquities (as described in the book) changed your view of your tribe's legacy?

2. How does the promise of blessings for "those yet to be born" inspire you to take action in the restoration process?

Small Group Discussion Questions

1. The chapter emphasizes God's justice against evil spirits. Discuss what "justice being served" means to you personally in the context of your family's spiritual journey.

2. The chapter describes a courtroom scene where evil spirits are judged. How does this imagery help you understand spiritual authority? What challenges might someone face in embracing this process?

3. As a group, discuss what a "restored bloodline" looks like in practical terms. How might families or communities live differently after a successful generational restoration?

ABOUT THE AUTHOR

Susan Bowman has ministered inner healing and deliverance for over twenty years. Year after year she watched sincere believers chase every promising method, only to see their breakthroughs slip away. Something was missing. Scripture kept pointing to the heart — *above all else, guard it*. Why the urgency? Neurocardiology supplied the answer: childhood moments literally etch a blueprint into the physical heart, a hidden script that silently controls every reaction to life's challenges. Susan wove Proverbs 4:23 together with Romans 10:10 — *for with the heart one believes* — and peer-reviewed science into a gentle, repeatable protocol. It doesn't patch symptoms; it rewrites the blueprint. Sustainable freedom is real — and it starts in the heart. Discover the tools at **www.thepoolministries.org**.

www.ingramcontent.com/pod-product-compliance
Lightning Source LLC
Chambersburg PA
CBHW052023070526
44584CB00016B/1868